GUITAR**FRETBOARD**
FLUENCY

Master Creative Guitar Soloing, Intervals, Scale Patterns & Sequences

JOSEPH**ALEXANDER**

FUNDAMENTAL**CHANGES**

Guitar Fretboard Fluency

2nd Edition

Master Creative Guitar Soloing, Intervals, Scale Patterns & Sequences

ISBN: 978-1-78933-061-8

Published by **www.fundamental-changes.com**

www.fundamental-changes.com

Twitter: @guitar_joseph

Over 10,000 fans on Facebook: **FundamentalChangesInGuitar**

Instagram: **FundamentalChanges**

For over 350 Free Guitar Lessons with Videos Check Out

www.fundamental-changes.com

Cover Image Copyright: ShutterStock: _EG_

Other Books from Fundamental Changes

Contents

Introduction

This book will help you master the guitar fretboard while learning the most important melodic patterns and soloing approaches used in modern music. Whatever style of music you play, **Guitar Fretboard Fluency** will open up the neck and put every essential scale instantly at your fingertips.

This book is broken into two parts. The first part explores the methods that guitarists use to create melody while building fluency and technique on the guitar. You will learn the sequential patterns, interval skips, triads and arpeggios that turn scales into usable melodic tools. This section, while greatly improving your technique will also heighten your creative and aural skills, because every single exercise teaches you melodic vocabulary that builds to give total creative freedom.

As musicians, one of the biggest challenges is that our fingers are often in charge of our brain. Patterns or licks we have memorised have a habit of coming out without us consciously meaning to play them. How many times have you thought, "Damn! I just played that same lick *again!*"?

Part One of this book will not only allow you to build *new* melodic ideas, it will help you to creatively apply these ideas in musical situations. It will help you break out of soloing ruts while developing fretboard knowledge, excellent technique, and a creative, conscious command of the guitar.

In Part One, you will learn many important ways to be creative with scales, and apply these approaches to the most common scale shapes on guitar. All five Major, Pentatonic, Melodic and Harmonic Minor scale shapes are covered so that your fingers are familiar with any pattern you may encounter.

You will learn useful, focused practice routines to help you get the most out of your time, and some important psychological tips to help you stay focused and positive.

Part One contains a great deal of melodic material on the guitar, and while you can use it to build devastating technique, you will find that the emphasis throughout is on developing your ears, your musicality and your own individual voice on the guitar. You can play these exercises as fast as you like, but the real benefit comes when you play slow.

Think of each pattern as an opportunity to teach your ears a new melody to use in many future solos. Play one note and sing the next before hitting it. Building this connection between your ears and fingers is what this book is all about.

Part Two of Fretboard Fluency is where you will get intimately acquainted with the guitar neck. The goal is to learn *every* important scale, in *every* key in *every* position on the fretboard. This may sound like a daunting task, and it will take a while to master this skill, but once you have mastered it then it will stay with you for life.

There are many scales in music, but 99% of the time modern musicians use just sixteen different scales to improvise with. Generally, rock and blues players will use fewer different scales, and jazz fusion players will use more.

These common scales are

- The seven modes of the Major scale

- Major and Minor Pentatonic scales

- Harmonic Minor and one of its modes

- Melodic Minor and two of its modes

- The Half Whole and Whole Tone scale

Some scales are much more commonly used than others, so the most important sounds are prioritised to get you making music quickly.

If you don't know what a mode is, or you haven't heard of a Melodic Minor scale, don't worry. There will be a brief theory primer in each section and plenty of opportunities to musically apply each scale. However, if these concepts are genuinely new to you, then I strongly suggest you pick up copies of **The Practical Guide to Modern Music Theory** and **Guitar Scales in Context** and read them in conjunction with each new scale's section.

Part Two begins with a quick look at how to memorise the notes on the fretboard using shapes and patterns to help you. While learning scales on the guitar is normally based on memorising shapes at first, it is vital that you know how to instantly locate the root note of the key in which you wish to play.

We then move on to learning how to play *any* scale in *any* key *anywhere* on the neck. This method is based on the CAGED system in which the five scale shapes you learned in Part One are linked to *anchor* chords.

All modes are derived from a single *parent scale.* By visualising the parent scale shape around a different anchor chord we can instantly access any mode we wish to play. To move the mode to a different key, all we need to do is move the anchor chord to a different root note. This is a powerful technique and is a big factor in opening up the fretboard.

By using these simple anchor chords and working in a few different keys, the guitar neck opens up extremely quickly. It may sound a little complex but I promise you it's a simple process.

Once again, useful and efficient practice routines are included to enable you to quickly master every scale and key.

Part 2 is carefully organised so that you learn the most common and useful scales first. Before launching into slightly more obscure scales, ask yourself how useful they are for the style of music that you play. You may be better off getting creative with the more common scales and patterns from earlier in the book.

I'm not trying to put you off learning the later scales (they're included for a reason!), but we have a limited amount of time in our lives to make music, so prioritise the scales that help you make the music you want to play.

There is no need to work through this book in order. In fact, I recommend you combine Parts One and Two of this book from the outset. You will practice effectively if you instantly apply melodic sequences and patterns in Part One to the scales and positions in Part Two. Throughout, there are suggested practice routines and any patterns and scales that I consider a priority are marked with a *.

This book is about training your hands to follow the musical ideas in your head, so it is important to download and listen to the free audio that comes with the book.

Get the Audio

The audio files for this book are available to download for free from **www.fundamental-changes.com** and the link is in the top right corner. Simply select this book title from the drop-down menu and follow the instructions to get the audio.

We recommend that you download the files directly to your computer, not to your tablet, and extract them there before adding them to your media library. You can then put them on your tablet, iPod or burn them to CD. On the download page there is a help PDF and we also provide technical support via the contact form.

Kindle / eReaders

To get the most out of this book, remember that you can double tap any image to enlarge it. Turn off 'column viewing' and hold your kindle in landscape mode.

For over 350 Free Guitar Lessons with Videos Check out:

www.fundamental-changes.com

Twitter: @guitar_joseph

FB: **FundamentalChangesInGuitar**

Instagram: **FundamentalChanges**

Part One: Sequences, Intervals, Triads and Arpeggios

Introduction to Part One

Most popular music is not made up of patterns, sequences and lines of intervallic skips. These ideas occur often in heavy rock or 'shred' guitar solos, but they are usually a short feature to build tension. If all solos were simply sequences of melodic patterns, they would get boring quite quickly.

Without wading into the age old (and pointless) 'technique versus feel' debate, my *opinion* is that guitar solos are often described as 'soulless' when they comprise mainly of the kind of patterns guitarists practice as technique exercises.

When a guitar solo is described as 'expressive' or a guitarist is described as having 'good feel', the musician has often still practiced patterns and scales, but their goal is of fretboard and musical freedom, rather than speed and technique.

Speed is a useful measuring stick. By increasing the metronome speed and playing a pattern accurately, we can easily measure tangible improvement and feel good about our progression. Unfortunately, the flip side of that coin is that by exhaustively working to increase speed on an exercise, we train our hands to *only* know that exercise. Any gains in technique are offset by new limits to our creativity. The idea of a guitar solo is to add something new to the music and take the song to a different place. How can we bring something new to a piece of music if our hands are 'locked' into playing just one or two patterns?

The solution is to ensure that we practice technical exercise in a creative, musical way, and to realise that the goal of this kind of practice is to teach our ears new melodic possibilities.

If most popular forms of music aren't built from sequences and 'angular' patterns, then why is it so important for us to practice them? I believe there are a few reasons.

- Confidence and fluency

Practising scales in melodic patterns, interval skips, triads and arpeggios makes us very confident of where the scale notes lie on the fingerboard. With this kind of confidence, we can play with conviction and feeling.

- Ear training

Working carefully through different melodic patterns and structures allows us to hear and internalise melodic possibilities that we were previously unaware of. By forcing ourselves to practice different things, our ear will remember and internalise many different sounds. We create a huge dictionary of melodic sounds we can use when improvising or writing. These naturally combine to form interesting music. Also, by practising these ideas in a creative setting (with backing tracks or a band, rather than just a metronome), we learn to *feel* how a scale choice or structure affects the mood of the music.

- Building creative spontaneity

By getting confident with scales and learning many melodic ideas, we gain the confidence to spontaneously play something new. Record your playing and listen back to it 24 hours later. Re-hearing an idea that came to you spontaneously in an improvised solo often becomes the seed of a new song or lick.

- Technique

There's no denying that practising patterns, intervals, triads and arpeggios quickly builds guitar technique. Working with a metronome or drum machine and increasing the speed of an exercise is an important factor for *internalising* a pattern. The tricky part is knowing when to stop practising technique and when to start making the exercise musical.

The practice routines in this section give suggested speeds, but these will vary depending on your tastes and style. Learning guitar technique is simply the pursuit of fluency, confidence and the ability to play the music you hear in your head. Speed may be a part of that, but it is not the ultimate goal.

Three-Notes-Per-String versus CAGED Scale Shapes

Most scales contain seven different notes which are in set locations on the fretboard. It is possible to play each pitch in more than one location and each note in different octaves. This means that the whole fretboard can be filled with just one scale.

For example, the seven notes in C Major (C D E F G A B) are located in the following places:

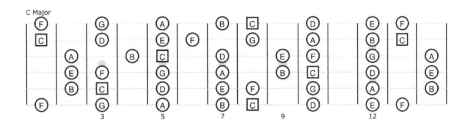

We need to break this large amount of information down into smaller chunks if we are to use it musically, and opinions are divided about how to do this.

Some players like to divide the parent scale into chunks that have three notes on each string and would, for example, divide up the notes between the fifth and ninth frets like this:

C Major

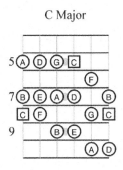

Other players divide this range up differently to avoid travelling too far away from the first note of the shape. Notice that in the following diagram the fourth fret is used and that the highest note is now a C, not a D as in the previous diagram.

C Major

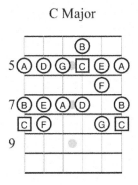

These smaller shapes are normally referred to as CAGED shapes because they are viewed as being built around one of the first open position chords you learn as a guitarist. These chords are the chords of C, A, G, E and D Major. The scale above is built around the shape of G Major.

C Major (G Shape)

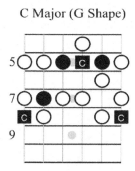

Three-notes-per-string scales lend themselves towards faster playing due to their uniformity, although it is easy to get locked into scale runs and patterns. They also lead to many melodies being phrased in groups of three due to their layout and make evenly grouped 1/16th or 1/8th note lines trickier to play.

CAGED shapes are more easily visualised around chord shapes. This makes 'target' notes and chord tones easier to find. They normally lie under the fingers more comfortably and do not require any position shifts. Large interval skips are often easier to play due to their smaller range, and even-note groupings are easier to phrase accurately. The downside is that the fingering change between the two- and three-note-per-string groupings can be challenging to control, so these shapes are not as easy to play at speed.

A major difference between the two systems is that (counter-intuitively) you need *seven* three-notes-per-string shapes to cover the fretboard but only *five* CAGED shapes to cover the whole fretboard.

My personal leaning is towards the mixed grouping (CAGED) scales as I play more jazz and blues, but when I was younger and played more technical rock music, I was heavily reliant on the three-notes-per-string shapes.

This book focuses on CAGED as I believe their many benefits outweigh their slight challenges. These scales fit perfectly into the CAGED system and are an excellent way to organise our thinking. However, I have also included diagrams for the three-notes-per-string shapes for the modes of the Major scale along the Melodic and Harmonic Minor modes in Appendix A.

The approaches in Part One can be applied to either type of scale shape, so use whichever you feel will suit your style of music better.

Chapter One: Melodic Sequences

This chapter teaches you the essential scale patterns and sequences that build fluency and melodic vocabulary on the guitar. They are initially taught in the first position of the Major scale before being applied to the other Major scale shapes and other scales.

Sequences are small, repeating melodic fragments that gradually ascend or descend a scale. These patterns teach your ears new melodic possibilities while building your technique, confidence and fluency.

Each pattern is taught around the following scale shape. Make sure you can play it fluently both ascending and descending before tackling the sequences in this chapter.

The root of the scale is shown with a square marker. Notice that this isn't always the lowest (bass) note of the scale.

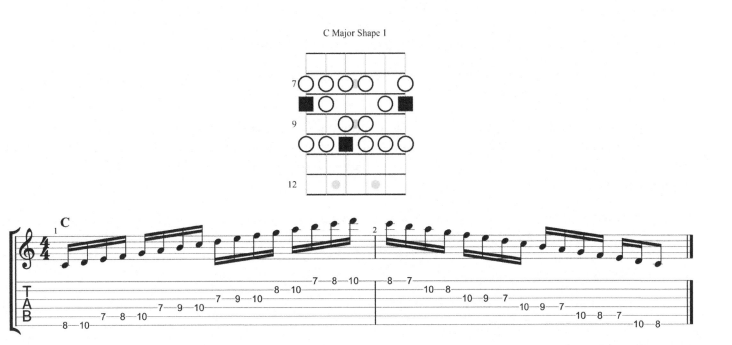

I've included a concise practice schedule that you should stick to when learning the sequences in this chapter. Once you have learnt the sequences it should take no more than five minutes each day to complete this routine.

You do *not* have to complete each exercise perfectly before you move on to the next. Set a timer for 30 second intervals and move on to the next exercise, even if you are not playing the current one to your satisfaction.

The reason for this strict approach is to make sure you are encountering as much melodic material as possible each day, and to teach you healthy practice habits.

Healthy Practice Habits

Imagine a scenario where I told you to choose the most difficult melodic pattern and play only that until you had it mastered at speed. It could take a few days to get it down and, even then, it may still be a bit shaky.

So now you've spent maybe three days working on just one pattern that you probably won't be confident enough to use musically and, more importantly, you've lost all that time you could have spent learning musical patterns that could have been easier or more useful.

Just because a pattern is harder, it doesn't mean it is more important or better. In fact, if a pattern is *really* hard, and you do spend a long time mastering just that, you will have trained your fingers to become locked into that pattern, so now it's all you can play. If you find something extremely difficult, you may not be ready for it yet. Maybe your technique needs a bit of work or maybe you don't know the scale well enough. If this is the case, learning easier patterns that you can quickly use musically will prepare you for more challenging ones later, and help you to learn the scale pattern more thoroughly.

Practising easier things first will help you feel more of a progression and associate positive, rather than negative feelings with your guitar.

When you have played through the complete schedule, stop and take a break for a few minutes. Then work on an exercise that uses one of the sequences in a creative way. These exercises are given in Chapter Five.

When the timer pings, always stop. Once again, this helps to build positive emotions when you play.

If you want to continue your practice after the timer goes, it's probably because it's either going really well or because it's frustrating you.

If your practice is going well and you decide to continue past your timer, you will eventually hit a point of frustration and put your guitar down. This means that you've left your guitar in a negative state and associated negative feelings with practice. Quit while you're feeling positive and you'll always come back to practice feeling enthused.

We all have days where practice doesn't go well and we get frustrated. The trick here is to be observant as to which *specific* things are challenging you. Keep working until the timer sounds, because sticking with something that is tough is an achievement in itself. After your practice, note down what was challenging you and take a break.

If you keep going after the timer finishes when you're frustrated, you will exhaust yourself mentally and be useless for the rest of the day. When it's time to practice again you will remember only negative feelings and avoid the guitar.

By stopping when the timer goes, even if you're frustrated, you have taken ownership of the task and kept control of the situation. You can approach the guitar later knowing that you're the boss. It's OK for things to be challenging, but know that there's no hurry to progress and that you are in control. You have isolated the specific thing that was frustrating you by writing it down, and you can come back and approach it on your terms when you're ready. In the meantime, work on the areas where you feel you're making progress.

This chapter contains eleven sequences that ascend and descend scales. The following table will help you to organise your time.

For the first few days, focus on learning all the patterns in position 1 of the Major scale, but on later days apply the patterns to all five shapes. Stick to the schedule and always move on when your timer pings.

Pattern	Day 1	Day 2	Day 3	Day 4	Day 5	Day 6	Day 7
A*	♫@60	♫@80	♫@100	𝅘𝅥𝅯𝅘𝅥𝅯𝅘𝅥𝅯𝅘𝅥𝅯 @50	𝅘𝅥𝅯𝅘𝅥𝅯𝅘𝅥𝅯𝅘𝅥𝅯 @75	𝅘𝅥𝅯𝅘𝅥𝅯𝅘𝅥𝅯𝅘𝅥𝅯 @90	𝅘𝅥𝅯𝅘𝅥𝅯𝅘𝅥𝅯𝅘𝅥𝅯 @100
B*	♫@60	♫@80	♫@100	𝅘𝅥𝅯𝅘𝅥𝅯𝅘𝅥𝅯𝅘𝅥𝅯 @50	𝅘𝅥𝅯𝅘𝅥𝅯𝅘𝅥𝅯𝅘𝅥𝅯 @75	𝅘𝅥𝅯𝅘𝅥𝅯𝅘𝅥𝅯𝅘𝅥𝅯 @90	𝅘𝅥𝅯𝅘𝅥𝅯𝅘𝅥𝅯𝅘𝅥𝅯 @100
C	♫@60	♫@80	♫@100	𝅘𝅥𝅯𝅘𝅥𝅯𝅘𝅥𝅯𝅘𝅥𝅯 @50	𝅘𝅥𝅯𝅘𝅥𝅯𝅘𝅥𝅯𝅘𝅥𝅯 @75	𝅘𝅥𝅯𝅘𝅥𝅯𝅘𝅥𝅯𝅘𝅥𝅯 @90	𝅘𝅥𝅯𝅘𝅥𝅯𝅘𝅥𝅯𝅘𝅥𝅯 @100
D*	♫@60	♫@80	♫@100	𝅘𝅥𝅯𝅘𝅥𝅯𝅘𝅥𝅯𝅘𝅥𝅯 @50	𝅘𝅥𝅯𝅘𝅥𝅯𝅘𝅥𝅯𝅘𝅥𝅯 @75	𝅘𝅥𝅯𝅘𝅥𝅯𝅘𝅥𝅯𝅘𝅥𝅯 @90	𝅘𝅥𝅯𝅘𝅥𝅯𝅘𝅥𝅯𝅘𝅥𝅯 @100
E	♫@60	♫@80	♫@100	𝅘𝅥𝅯𝅘𝅥𝅯𝅘𝅥𝅯𝅘𝅥𝅯 @50	𝅘𝅥𝅯𝅘𝅥𝅯𝅘𝅥𝅯𝅘𝅥𝅯 @75	𝅘𝅥𝅯𝅘𝅥𝅯𝅘𝅥𝅯𝅘𝅥𝅯 @90	𝅘𝅥𝅯𝅘𝅥𝅯𝅘𝅥𝅯𝅘𝅥𝅯 @100
F*	♫@60	♫@80	triplet@100	𝅘𝅥𝅯𝅘𝅥𝅯𝅘𝅥𝅯𝅘𝅥𝅯 @50	𝅘𝅥𝅯𝅘𝅥𝅯𝅘𝅥𝅯𝅘𝅥𝅯 @75	𝅘𝅥𝅯𝅘𝅥𝅯𝅘𝅥𝅯𝅘𝅥𝅯 @90	𝅘𝅥𝅯𝅘𝅥𝅯𝅘𝅥𝅯𝅘𝅥𝅯 @100
G*	triplet@60	triplet@80	triplet@100	sextuplet@50	sextuplet@60	sextuplet@70	sextuplet@80
H*	triplet@60	triplet@80	triplet@100	sextuplet@50	sextuplet@60	sextuplet@70	sextuplet@80
I*	triplet@60	triplet@80	triplet@100	sextuplet@50	sextuplet@60	sextuplet@70	sextuplet@80
J	triplet@60	triplet@80	triplet@100	sextuplet@50	sextuplet@60	sextuplet@70	sextuplet@80
K	triplet@60	triplet@80	triplet@100	sextuplet@50	sextuplet@60	sextuplet@70	sextuplet@80

* = Priority

This may seem a time-consuming task, but as your skills develop each example will only take a few seconds to play. You will eventually be able to ascend and descend through each example in this chapter in under four minutes when playing 1/16th notes at 90bpm. There are hints on how to develop speed later.

Don't worry if you don't reach the required speed each day, these ideas take time to master. Keep track of the tempo at which you can play each exercise and start a few bpm below that point each day. Also, focus only on the asterisked (*) exercises as these are the most important ones to master.

In the following sequences, only the first two bars of each ascending and descending pattern are shown. If the full exercise was written out for each sequence, this book would sink a battleship! Look at this as an opportunity to improve the connection between your brain and your ears. If you really get stuck towards the top of the scale, you can cheat by reading the descending version backwards.

Two bars is enough time to get the pattern into your ears and your fretboard skills will benefit greatly by using your ears to continue the sequence through the rest of the scale shapes.

The following exercises can be played over any chord sequence in the key of C. You can use backing track one while you practice.

Example 1a: * Run of 4, then back to +1 from previous start

1, 2, 3, 4 → 2, 3, 4, 5 → 3, 4, 5, 6

Example 1b: * 1, 2, 3, 1 → 2, 3, 4, 2 → etc

Example 1c: 1, 2, -1, 1 → 2, 3, 1, 2 → 3, 4, 2, 3

Example 1d: * 3, 1, 2 3 → 4, 2, 3 4 → 5, 3, 4, 5

Example 1e: 3, 2, 1, 3 → 4, 3, 2, 4 | → 5, 4, 3, 5

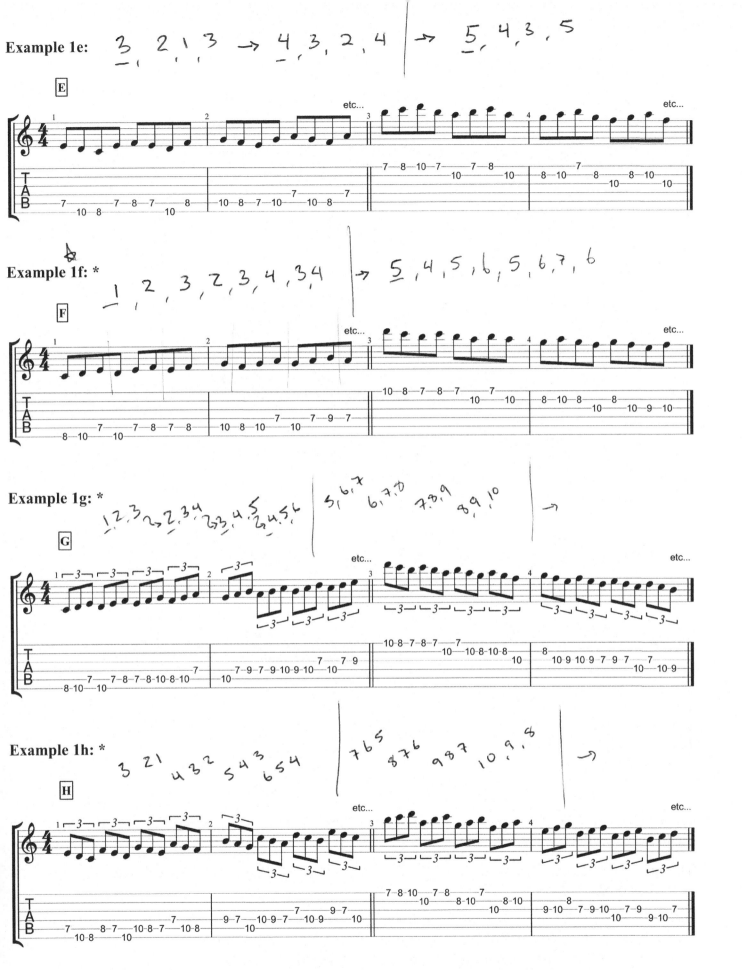

Example 1f: * 1, 2, 3, 2, 3, 4, 3, 4 | → 5, 4, 5, 6, 5, 6, 7, 6

Example 1g: * 1 2 3, 2 3 4, 3 4 5, 4 5 6 | 5, 6, 7 6, 7, 8 7, 8, 9 8, 9, 10 | →

Example 1h: * 3 2 1 4 3 2 5 4 3 6 5 4 | 7 6 5 8 7 6 9 8 7 10 9 8 | →

17

Example 1i: *

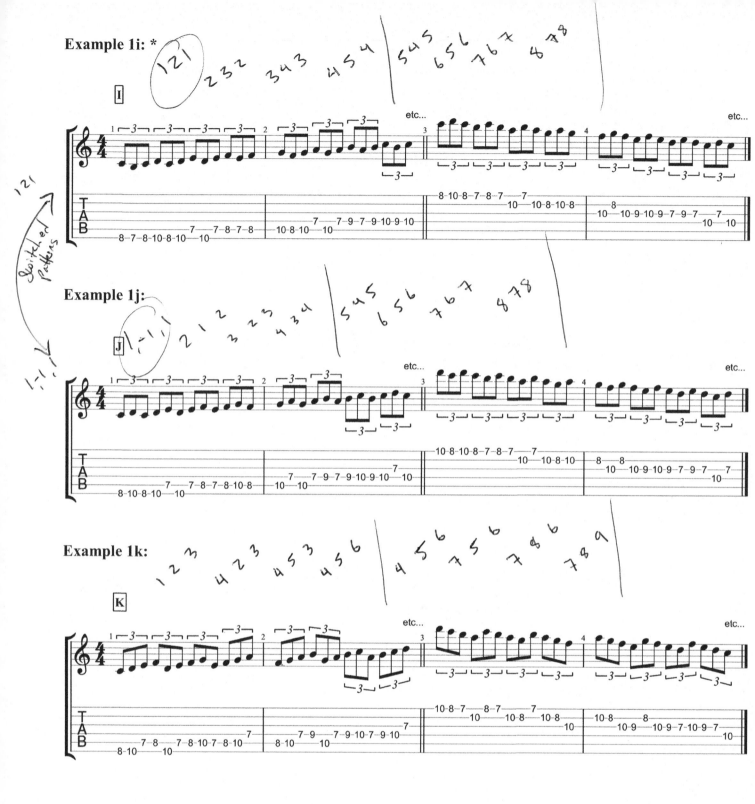

When you feel you have mastered one or two patterns, flick forward to Chapter Five and use the patterns with the musical creativity exercises.

The next step is to apply these patterns to the other four C Major scale shapes below to develop the same level of fluency in all positions.

In Part Two, you will learn how to use these five shapes to easily play any Major mode, so building familiarity now will be beneficial to you. All seven modes of the Major scale are played using these shapes, so the benefits of any practice you do here will be multiplied by seven times later.

The five shapes of the Major modes can be played as follows:

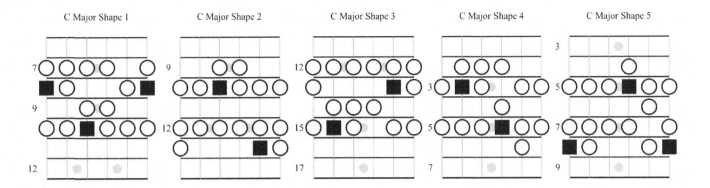

The following example demonstrates how to apply any pattern you know to a different scale shape.

Here is the melodic sequence from Example 1a:

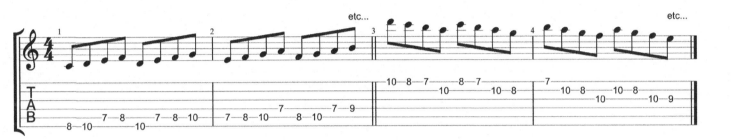

You should already know how to play this pattern well in shape 1, so it's not too hard to apply it to shape 2. If you prefer to read the notation part, make sure you take a quick look at the tablature to see where this sequence is played.

The pattern from Example 1a is played in shape 2 in the following way:

Example 1l:

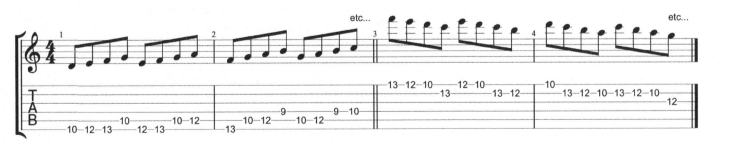

Repeat this process for all the other shapes.

There are a few ways you can organise your practice. My advice is to take just one sequence through all five shapes before moving on to the next, rather than applying all the sequences to one shape before moving on.

This may seem like a huge amount of work but it is simpler than you think. By focusing on one melodic sequence and applying it to all the shapes, the contour of the melody will quickly get into your ears and you will start to feel your way easily through each new shape. Of course, it helps if you spend some time memorising each of the five scale shapes before applying the sequences.

The following table will help to organise your practice with each scale shape and pattern.

Pattern	Day 1	Day 2	Day 3	Day 4	Day 5	Day 6	Day 7
A	All Shapes	x (rest)	All Shapes	x	All Shapes	x	All Shapes
B	All Shapes	x	All Shapes	x	All Shapes	x	All Shapes
C	All Shapes	x	All Shapes	x	All Shapes	x	All Shapes
D	x	All Shapes	x	All Shapes	All Shapes	x	All Shapes
E	x	All Shapes	x	All Shapes	All Shapes	x	All Shapes
F	x	All Shapes	x	All Shapes	All Shapes	x	All Shapes
G	x	x	All Shapes	x	x	All Shapes	All Shapes
H	x	x	All Shapes	x	x	All Shapes	All Shapes
I	x	x	All Shapes	x	x	All Shapes	All Shapes
J	x	x	x	All Shapes	x	All Shapes	All Shapes
K	x	x	x	All Shapes	x	All Shapes	All Shapes

It is important to consciously use these patterns in your improvisational practice too. Scale knowledge and fluency is important, but remember that the purpose of any technical exercise is to enable your musicality. Take your favourite sequences and use them with the exercises in Chapter Five.

Using these sequential ideas in your solos will sound forced and unnatural at first, and they will stick out like a sore thumb. However, with continued practice, they will gradually become a natural and integral part of your melodic vocabulary.

Building Speed and Fluency

Each sequence and pattern in this book is written as 1/8th notes for clarity and convenience, but they can be 'doubled-up' and played as 1/16th notes. The following steps will help you to both increase the metronome speed, and introduce 1/16th notes into your playing.

Begin with the following sequence:

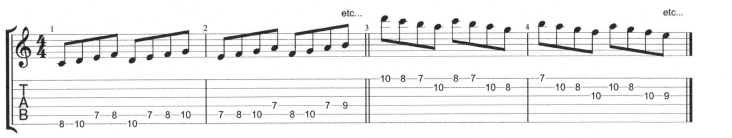

Ensure you can play this example cleanly at 60bpm before attempting the following steps.

Set the metronome to 60bpm and record yourself playing through the example four times.

Listen to your recording. If the notes are evenly spaced across the beat, increase the metronome by 8bpm.

When you reach 100bpm, halve the metronome speed to 50bpm but double the speed of the notes. You are now playing 1/16th notes at 50bpm. This is the same speed as 1/8th notes at 100bpm.

Example 1m: (example A played as 16th notes)

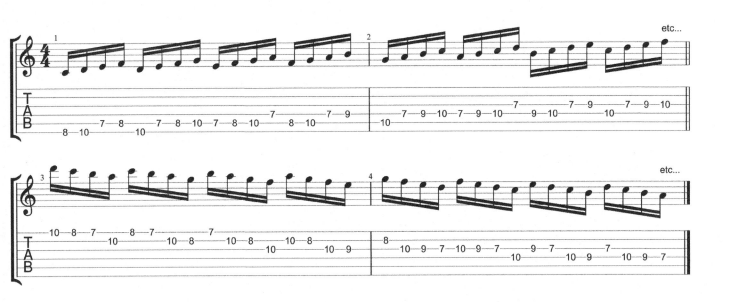

From 50bpm, try gradually raising the metronome speed again until you reach around 100-120bpm.

Play through each example every day rather than spending weeks trying to get one exercise ridiculously fast.

This method will build speed and technique extremely quickly. Remember, the ultimate goal is building the connection between your ears and the melody by developing confidence and fluency at a reasonable speed.

As your skills develop, each example will only take a few seconds to play. You will be able to ascend and descend through every example in this chapter in under four minutes when you play 1/16th notes at 90bpm.

Tap your foot. It might sound simple, but making the pulse a physical movement of your body makes you play more accurately. If you can't tap your foot accurately at first, slow the beat right down and practice carefully until you can.

Remember, don't let the pursuit of speed get in the way of the true goal of ear training. Every day, slow right down, play one note and then sing the next note in the sequence before picking it. This exercise has more far-reaching benefits for your musicianship and connection with your instrument than the pursuit of speed.

You can download the audio for free here:

www.fundamental-changes.com/download-audio

Chapter Two: Intervals

An interval is the name of the distance between two notes. The distance from C to D is a 2nd. The distance from C to E is a 3rd. Playing in intervals instead of running up and down scales is an important way to introduce jumps and leaps into melodies. These jumps can be small, such as a 3rd, or they can be large like a 6th.

Interval practice is useful for building guitar technique because playing larger leaps involves skipping strings and awkward fingerings. However, the real benefit is aural. Guitarists often practice by running up and down scales, and in doing so train their ears to hear only linear melodies. By forcing ourselves to introduce intervallic leaps into our practice, we train our ears to hear new melodic ideas, which then feed through into our natural playing. Remember, you are what you practice.

An interval can be played either ascending or descending and these directions can be combined into sequences. For example, the first interval skip could ascend and the next one could descend. Long patterns of these permutations can be strung together. This is shown in Example 2j where a sequence of two ascending 3rds and then a descending 3rd is played.

It is also possible to alter the rhythm of these patterns. Playing two-note interval patterns in triplets creates interesting cross-rhythmic effects.

Start by learning the basic interval skip patterns from 3rds all the way through to octaves. Use the following routine to organise your practice time.

Pattern	Day 1	Day 2	Day 3	Day 4	Day 5	Day 6	Day 7
A*	♫@60	♫@80	♫@100	♬♬@50	♬♬@75	♬♬@90	♬♬@100
B*	♫@60	♫@80	♫@100	♬♬@50	♬♬@75	♬♬@90	♬♬@100
C	♫@60	♫@80	♫@100	♬♬@50	♬♬@75	♬♬@90	♬♬@100
D*	♫@60	♫@80	♫@100	♬♬@50	♬♬@75	♬♬@90	♬♬@100
E	♫@60	♫@80	♫@100	♬♬@50	♬♬@75	♬♬@90	♬♬@100
F	♫@60	♫@80	♫@100	♬♬@50	♬♬@75	♬♬@90	♬♬@100

Example 2a: *

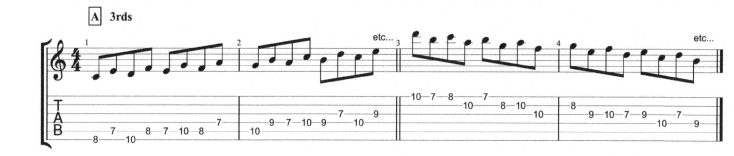

Example 2b: *

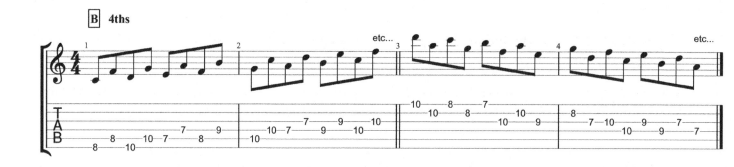

Example 2c:

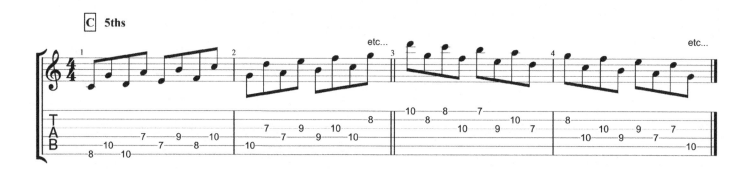

Example 2d: *

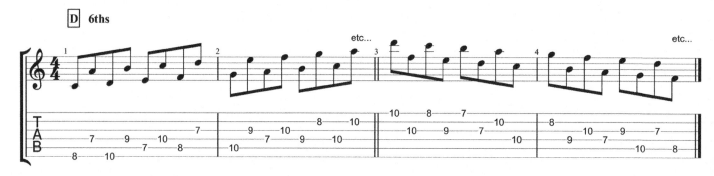

Example 2e:

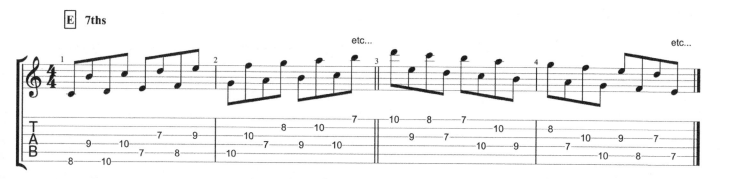

Example 2f:

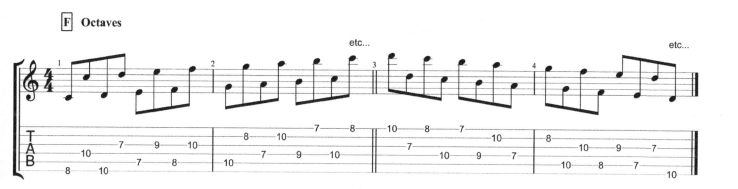

It is possible to combine interval skips in different directions to create interesting melodic ideas. By reversing intervals and combining groups of three or more skips into a sequence, we access a wide range of musical possibilities. These exercises dramatically increase our familiarity with the scale shape and build confidence and fluency in our soloing.

The following patterns, permutations and rhythmic variations are all based around the interval of a 3rd, but you must also learn these sequences with the other interval skips (4ths, 5ths and 6ths etc.). I suggest that you spend a week learning the following examples with 3rds before moving on to using each melodic idea with a different interval.

Use the following table to help you efficiently organise your practice.

Pattern	Day 1	Day 2	Day 3	Day 4	Day 5	Day 6	Day 7
G*	♫@60	♫@80	♫@100	♬@50	♬@75	♬@90	♬@100
H*	♫@60	♫@80	♫@100	♬@50	♬@75	♬@90	♬@100
I	♫@60	♫@80	♫@100	♬@50	♬@75	♬@90	♬@100
J*	♫@60	♫@80	♫@100	♬@50	♬@75	♬@90	♬@100
K	♫@60	♫@80	♫@100	♬@50	♬@75	♬@90	♬@100
L*	♪³♪@60	♪³♪@80	♪³♪@100	♬⁶♬@50	♬⁶♬@60	♬⁶♬@70	♬⁶♬@80
M*	♪³♪@60	♪³♪@80	♪³♪@100	♬⁶♬@50	♬⁶♬@60	♬⁶♬@70	♬⁶♬@80

Example 2g: (inverted 3rds) *

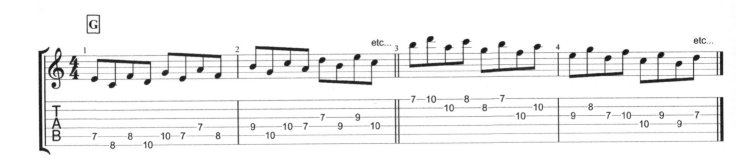

Example 2h: (one up, one down) *

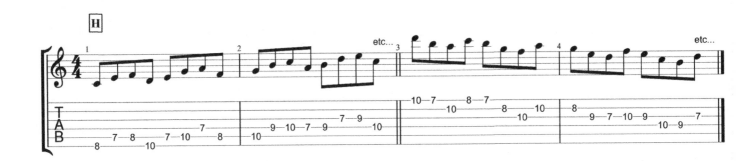

Example 2i: (one down, one up)

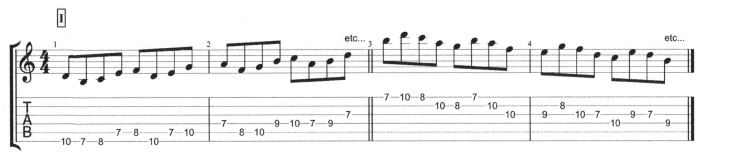

Example 2j: (two up, one down) *

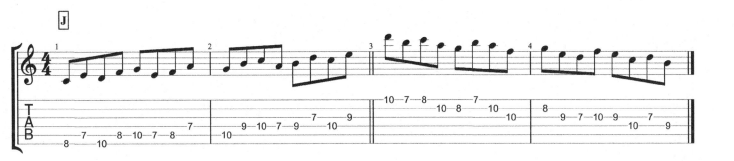

Example 2k: (two down, one up)

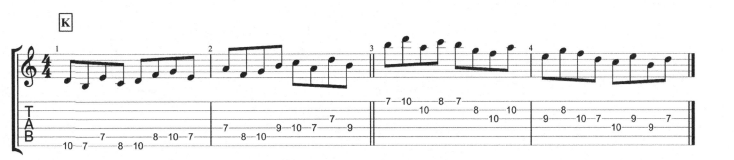

Example 2l: (in triplets – 2 against 3 feel) *

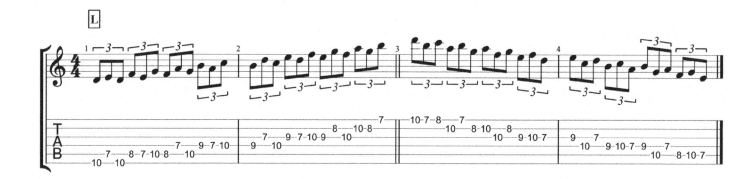

Example 2m: (one up, one down in triplets. 6 against 3 feel) *

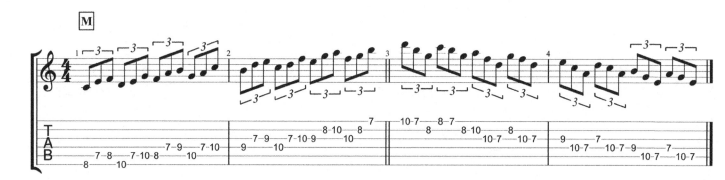

All of these ideas can and should be applied to the other intervals. For example, here is Example 2g played with 4ths:

Example 2n: (inverted 4ths)

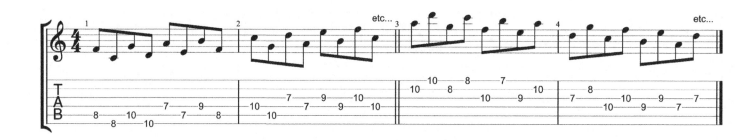

Use the following table to plan your practice over the period of a few weeks. As you progress you will find that you only need to briefly recap earlier intervals so you can spend more time working on the trickier sequences. This routine may not be perfect for you, so keep track of your own progress and prioritise the intervals and sequences you like the most.

Pattern	Day 1	Day 2	Day 3	Day 4	Day 5	Day 6	Day 7
G	4ths ♫	4ths ♬♬	5ths ♫	6ths ♫	6ths ♬♬	7ths ♫	8ths ♫
H	4ths ♫	4ths ♬♬	5ths ♫	6ths ♫	6ths ♬♬	7ths ♫	8ths ♫
I	4ths ♫	4ths ♬♬	5ths ♫	6ths ♫	6ths ♬♬	7ths ♫	8ths ♫
J	4ths ♫	4ths ♬♬	5ths ♫	6ths ♫	6ths ♬♬	7ths ♫	8ths ♫
K	4ths ♫	4ths ♬♬	5ths ♫	6ths ♫	6ths ♬♬	7ths ♫	8ths ♫
L	4ths ♫³	4ths ♬♬♬⁶	5ths ♫³	6ths ♫³	6ths ♬♬♬⁶	7ths ♫³	8ths ♫³
M	4ths ♫³	4ths ♬♬♬⁶	5ths ♫³	6ths ♫³	6ths ♬♬♬⁶	7ths ♫³	8ths ♫³

When you have developed an understanding of how these melodic structures work in position 1 of the Major scale, apply them to the other four shapes of the Major scale.

As soon as you have built confidence with one idea, use it with the creative practice ideas in Chapter Five.

Chapter Three: Triads

Stacking two intervals of a 3rd on top of each other forms a triad:

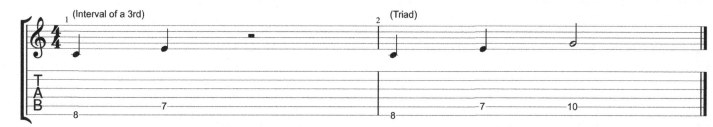

Dividing scales using triads is more challenging than using 3rds because we must visualise and hear two notes in advance instead of one. There is the potential for many melodic permutations of triad sequences as we now have three notes in each sequence.

This book isn't about mathematical possibilities, so the following examples are the most useful and *musical* applications of triads. I suggest sticking to these, although if you have a lot of spare time you may wish to explore further after finishing this book.

Even though these triads are formed from two stacked 3rds, there is no particular reason why you can't stack 4ths or 5ths. These ideas are well outside the scope of this book, but if you have an enquiring, mathematical mind, these permutations could be something to investigate. A word of warning though, *keep the end goal of making music in mind.*

The approaches in this book are useful and musical. When you start exploring stacked 4ths and 5ths etc., the melodies you create become angular and disjointed. Music has been based on scales, intervals, triads and arpeggios for hundreds of years, so I advise mastering this common vocabulary before launching into a career of experimental fusion!

As triads are three-note structures they are often learnt in triplets. Playing triplets is useful at first, however a lot of interesting patterns can be made with 'even' 1/8th note or 1/16th note rhythms. It is also possible to play four notes in a triad sequence, as you will see in Example 3o. By playing one of the notes in the triad twice, we create a wide variety of interesting melodies.

Example 3a: (ascending) *

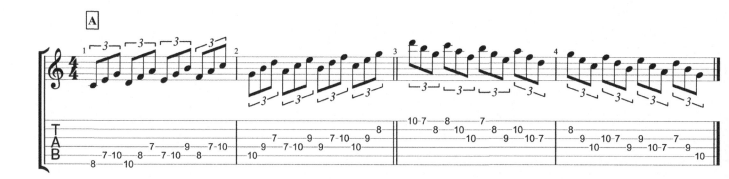

Example 3b: (descending) *

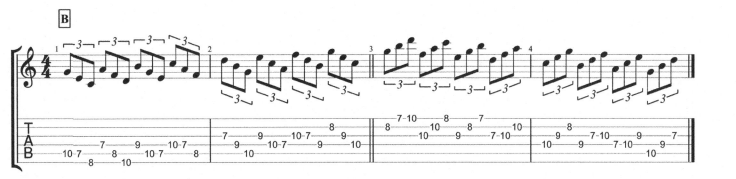

Example 3c: (combined) *

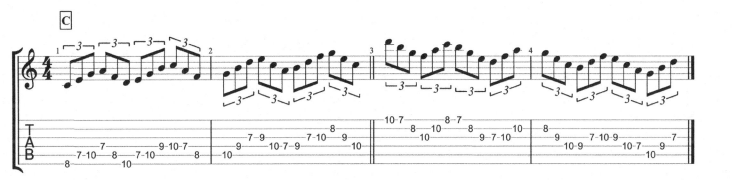

Example 3d: (high, low, middle) *

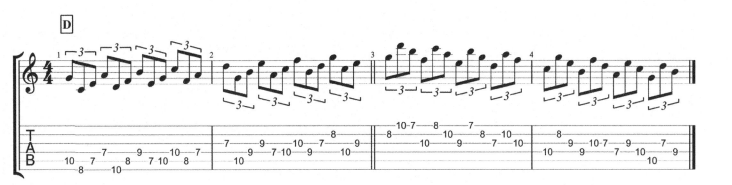

Example 3e: (middle, high, low)

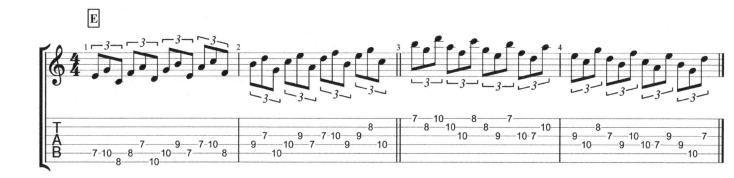

Example 3f: (four note pattern, lowest note doubled) *

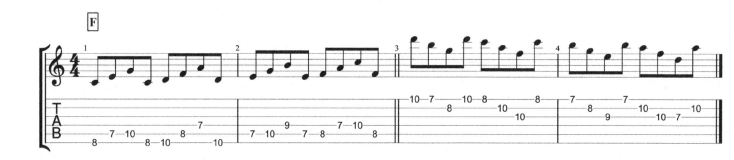

Example 3g: (four note pattern, middle note doubled)

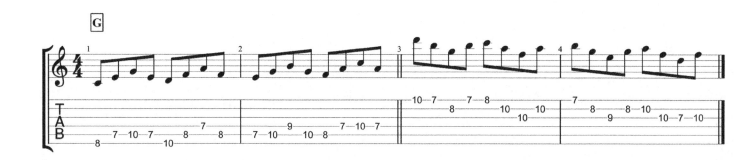

Example 3h: (four note pattern, lowest note doubled)

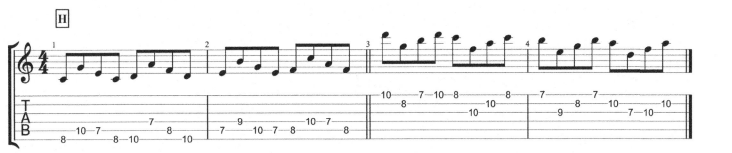

Example 3i: (four note pattern, middle note doubled)

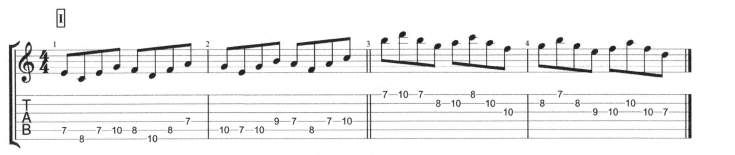

Example 3j: (four note pattern, top note doubled) *

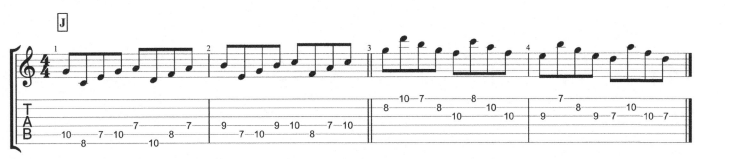

Example 3k: (ascending 3 against 2 feel) *

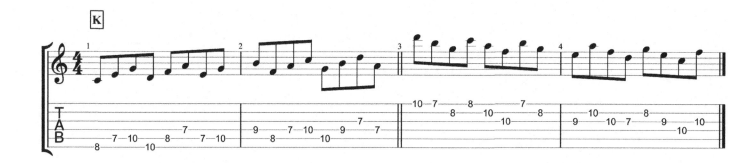

Example 3l: (descending 3 against 2 feel)

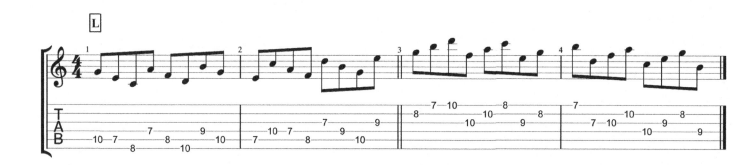

Example 3m: (combined 3 against 2 feel)

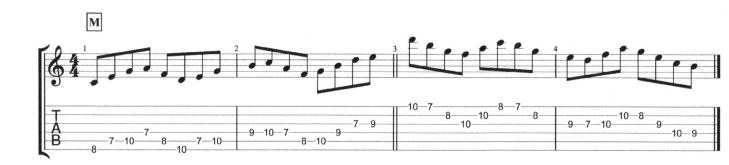

Example 3n: (reversed combined 3 against 2 feel)

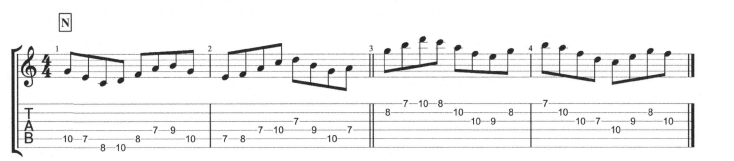

It is possible to stack 4ths and other intervals into triad-like structures. These ideas can be worth exploring, but your mileage may vary!

The following example shows you how to stack 4ths into triad-like structures:

Example 3o:

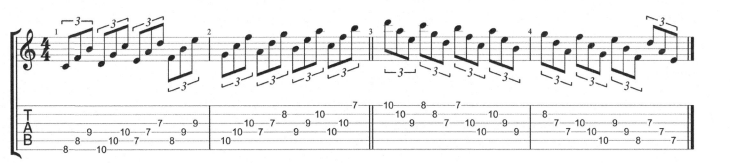

When you being to master triad patterns in shape 1, transfer them to the other four shapes. You will find that your fretboard fluency increases dramatically with a little effort. Due to their wide intervallic leaps, triplets are one of the best scale divisions to practice in order to build technique, fluency and vision on the guitar.

Once again, it is extremely important to spend time incorporating triplet ideas into your playing. This is done via deliberate creative practice, so once you have a good command of one or two of the triplet ideas, use the techniques in Chapter Five to help you bring them into your natural playing.

Chapter Four: Arpeggios

When you have gained confidence with triads, the next step is to study how to use arpeggio (four-note) structures to break up scales. Just like triads, arpeggios are formed by stacking 3rds on top of each other.

Arpeggios are formed by stacking three 3rds:

The distance between the first and final note of an arpeggio forms the interval of a 7th. Because of the larger jumps, arpeggios are more technically challenging to play than triads. Often the next note in the sequence is some distance away on the fretboard and because of this, your scale knowledge, insight and technique will increase dramatically when working through these patterns.

By adding one extra note to a triad, the number of available sequence patterns in an arpeggio is greatly increased. It is of course possible to explore every possible arrangement of these four notes with both 1/8th notes and triplets, but the truth is that not every permutation is useful. The following patterns are the ones that I believe to be useful, immediate and musical, but your ears may feel differently. Once you have got most of the arpeggio patterns under your fingers, feel free to experiment and find new possibilities.

As the following arpeggio patterns are challenging, work slowly through each one. The most important arpeggio patterns are asterisked, so concentrate on mastering these and using them creatively before working on the more difficult and unusual permutations.

Remember that these patterns are not only here to train your fingers and build fretboard fluency, they are designed to open your ears to new melodic possibilities. While speed and fluency are useful goals and can help to measure your progress, a more musical goal would be to work on incorporating these ideas into improvisations and naturally bringing them into your playing.

Four-note arpeggio sequences tend to be more common in jazz and fusion music, but even if you're not into these musical styles, practising arpeggio sequences is one of the best ways to get inside a scale shape. You are forced to visualise and hear large musical distances that will truly test your knowledge of the scale until you know its shape like the back of your hand.

As with all the structures in this book, as soon as you begin to master a sequence in shape 1, transfer the sequence to the other four Major scale patterns.

The following table will help to efficiently organise your practice time.

Pattern	Day 1	Day 2	Day 3	Day 4	Day 5	Day 6	Day 7
A*	♫@60	♫@70	♫@80	♬@50	♬@60	♬@70	♬@80
B*	♫@60	♫@70	♫@80	♬@50	♬@60	♬@70	♬@80
C	♫@60	♫@70	♫@80	♬@50	♬@60	♬@70	♬@80
D	♫@60	♫@70	♫@80	♬@50	♬@60	♬@70	♬@80
E	♫@60	♫@70	♫@80	♬@50	♬@60	♬@70	♬@80
F	♫@60	♫@70	♫@80	♬@50	♬@60	♬@70	♬@80
G*	♪³@60	♪³@70	♪³@80	♬⁶@50	♬⁶@55	♬⁶@60	♬⁶@65
H*	♪³@60	♪³@70	♪³@80	♬⁶@50	♬⁶@55	♬⁶@60	♬⁶@65
I*	♪³@60	♪³@70	♪³@80	♬⁶@50	♬⁶@55	♬⁶@60	♬⁶@65
J	♪³@60	♪³@70	♪³@80	♬⁶@50	♬⁶@55	♬⁶@60	♬⁶@65

Example 4a: (ascending) *

Example 4b: (descending) *

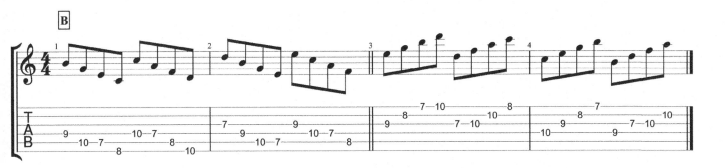

Example 4c: (ascend then descend)

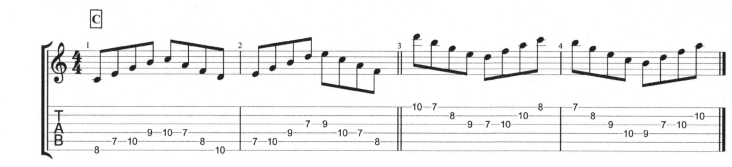

Example 4d: (descend then ascend)

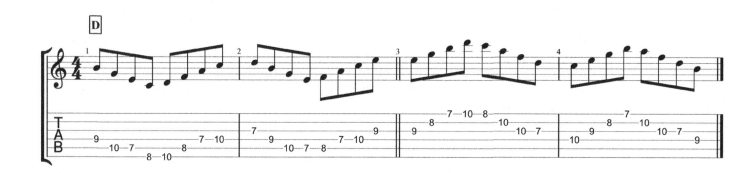

Example 4e: (Low to high then descend)

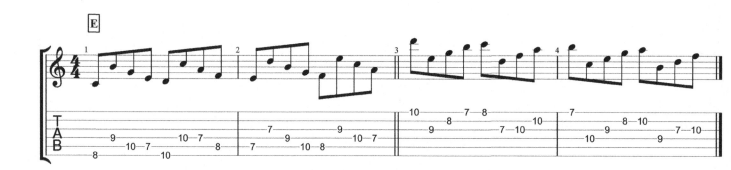

Example 4f: (descend then jump)

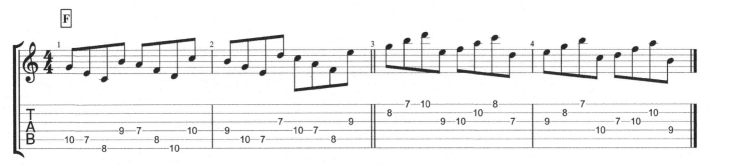

Example 4g: (4 against 3 feel ascending) *

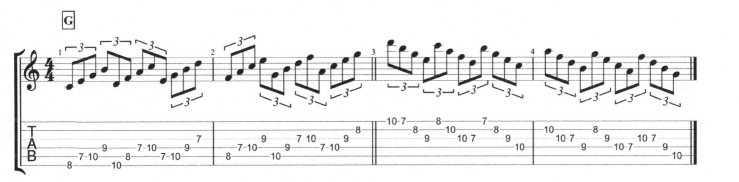

Example 4h: (4 against 3 feel descending) *

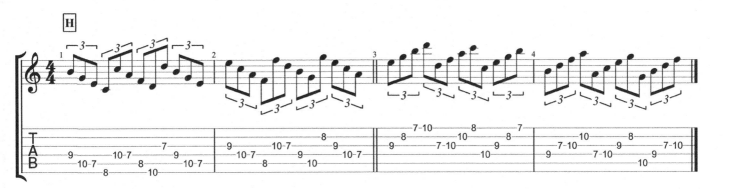

Example 4i: (4 against 3 feel ascending then descending) *

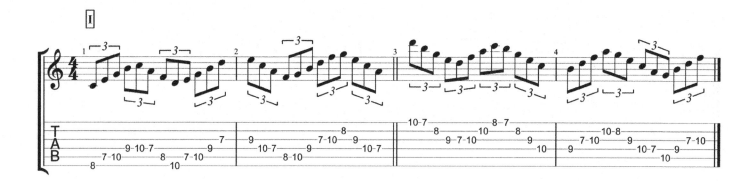

Example 4j: (4 against 3 feel descending then ascending)

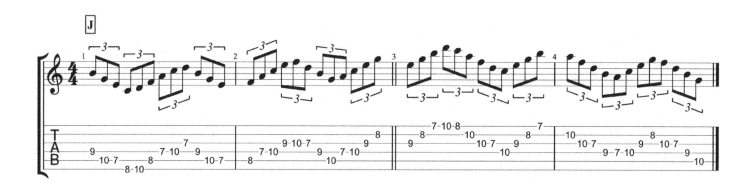

Arpeggio patterns are challenging for your technique but they greatly improve your fretboard fluency.

Chapter Five: Creative Practice

Learning and using new vocabulary in any language can be difficult, and music is no exception. There is always an awkward moment where new phrases are first used in conversation. They always sound obvious and unnatural at first.

The secret to progression, whether in language or in music, is to *force* yourself to apply new words to your existing speech. While these new phrases will stand out at first, they will quickly become a natural part of your language. The more often you practice incorporating new phrases into your music, the easier this process will become.

In this chapter, we look at how to incorporate the melodic structures from previous chapters into your playing, and how to use them as a springboard to create new and interesting melodies.

There is no 'correct' way to incorporate new melodic structures into your playing so that they sound natural, but if I were forced to give a routine, it would look something like this:

1. Over a backing track, play a strong, simple 'set up' phrase

2. Play a *short* fragment of a pre-determined melodic structure that begins on a chord tone

3. Resolve the structure in any way that feels natural and musical

By beginning with a set musical phrase, we do not have to worry about how to begin the creative process and can reliably 'set up' the second step.

Step two is where the chosen melodic structure is used. Stick with one idea at a time and try to keep the pattern fairly short. At first, begin the structure or pattern on a chord tone of the tonic key. For example, in the key of C, begin the line on the note C, E or G. When you become used to using a specific pattern, you can start to alter the rhythm and phrasing of the line.

After a few beats of playing the structure, resolve it in any way that feels natural. Trust your ears at this point. By not worrying about how the line will resolve you reduce the pressure on yourself to make it work perfectly. Gradually, your ear will improve and you will find resolutions more easily.

We will work in the key of C using backing track two. To keep things simple, we will use the melodic sequence from Example 1a, although this approach should obviously be applied to any sequence, interval, triad or arpeggio pattern.

Make sure you are familiar with this sequence before moving on.

Now that you know which melodic structure you will use, put on backing track two and play a short, simple lick to use at the start of the practice routine. Pentatonic licks are good at this point. To get you started, try the following line:

Example 5a:

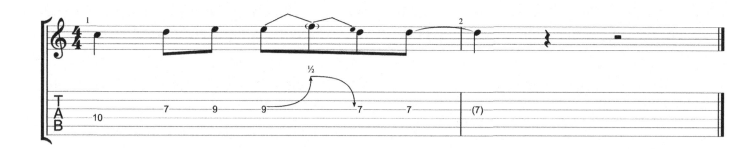

You now know how you will begin the practice routine.

Over backing track two play the above lick and then play a *short* fragment of the melodic sequence beginning from a chord tone. In this case, the sequence begins from the root, C. Resolve the line in any way that seems appropriate.

Example 5b:

As you can see, only a short portion of the sequence has been used, and while it may seem a little forced, this is how to consciously bring patterns like this into your playing.

Use the same line a few times and find different ways to resolve it before exploring the same sequence beginning from a different point in the scale.

Example 5c:

As you can see, there are an unlimited number of places where you can start or finish this type of sequence. Your placement will very much depend on the lick that you use to begin the improvisation, and what chords are playing in the background.

Come up with your own starting lick and play with different styles of backing tracks while sticking to the same melodic sequence idea. Make sure you play in different areas of the fretboard.

Be organised and methodical in your practice and stick with one melodic sequence for a few days before moving on to the next. This way, you will find plenty of ways to incorporate the pattern naturally into your playing.

The next stage is to experiment with the *rhythm* of the melodic sequence. There is no need to play a set rhythm in a sequence, and by breaking it up with longer notes you will train your ears to improvise with any pattern.

Using a similar idea to Example 5b, notice how I use different rhythms to break up the phrase:

Example 5d:

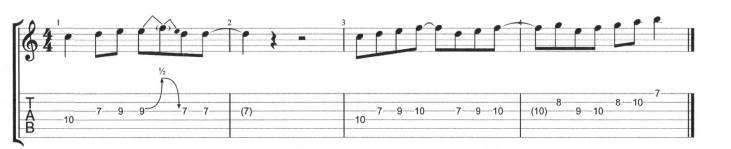

The rhythm of a melodic pattern can be broken up in any way imaginable. If you feel that the rhythm causes you to vary the pattern, then go with it. Remember, the whole point of these melodic structures is to teach your ears to hear different musical ideas, not to get stuck in patterns.

The following line is an unplanned, rhythmically-altered variation of the sequence that then morphs into a whole new idea.

Example 5e:

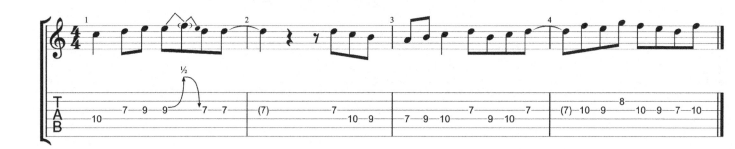

Another important idea is to *displace* the sequence so that it begins either before or after the beat.

Example 5f: (early)

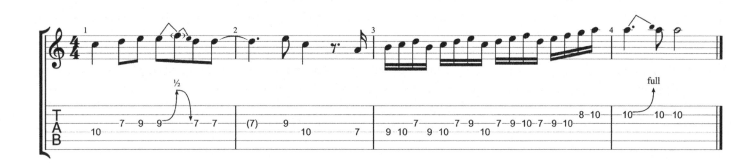

Example 5g: (late)

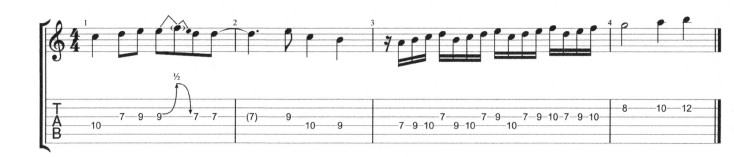

Experiment by picking certain notes in the pattern more than once. By doing this you will naturally displace and alter the sequence, and this leads to some unique melodic phrases.

Example 5h:

One way to create more elaborate ideas is to combine different kinds of melodic structure. For example, we could mix the previous sequence with another structure such as 3rds.

This line uses an idea from Example 2a.

Example 5i:

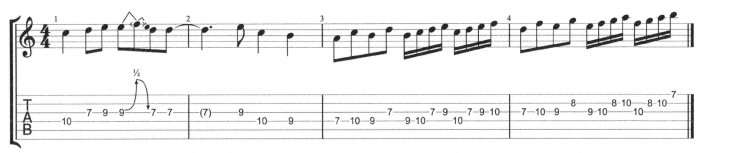

Try adding a large melodic leap to the end of any scale sequence. Here is just one of millions of possibilities.

Example 5j:

There are many other approaches you can take to explore these ideas creatively, but the ideas in this chapter give you a good starting point. They can be applied to any scale, interval, triad or arpeggio pattern from the previous four chapters.

The key is to have a defined starting point, and to only introduce a small fragment of a melodic sequence at a time.

Explore these ideas beginning on every note of the scale.

Chapter Six: Application to Other Scales

Until now, this book has focused on learning melodic patterns and developing fretboard skills with the five shapes of the Major scale. There are, however, two other seven-note 'parent' scales that derive different modes. These are the Melodic Minor scale and Harmonic Minor scale.

It may sound daunting to think of another set of seven modes for each of the Melodic and Harmonic Minor scales but fortunately only a few of these modes are commonly used outside of modern jazz or fusion. Of course, if fusion is your preferred style, the modes of these scales may be of interest. There are some great books on Melodic Minor theory and I highly encourage you to explore these interesting sounds in a creative environment.

Although you will probably only use the parent scales and a few of their modes, it is essential to master these shapes all over the neck, just as you did with the Major scale shapes. Once again, the seven modes of each minor scale are derived from the parent scales. As with the Major scale there are five scale patterns to learn for each Minor scale. You will learn how to use these shapes to create different modes in Part Two.

It is also extremely important to explore the Minor Pentatonic scale, as it is the most commonly used scale in modern blues, pop and rock music. While it does not form traditional modes, many players often only feel at home in only one or two of its positions. The approaches in the previous chapters can easily be adapted to fit the Minor Pentatonic scale, especially the sequential and intervallic ideas.

Minor Pentatonic Scale Shapes

We will begin by exploring the Minor Pentatonic scale and see how we can use the earlier approaches to get to know it better. As the Minor Pentatonic scale contains only five notes, we must think a little differently when using these approaches, although with the seven-note Melodic and Harmonic Minor scales, the previous concepts can be applied directly.

In the key of C, the five Minor Pentatonic scale shapes are as follows:

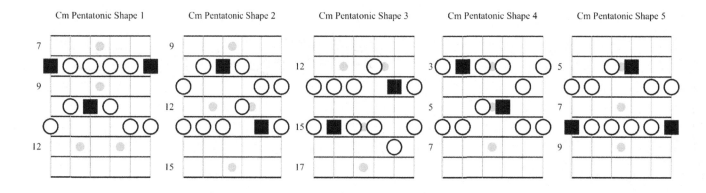

Joined together on the neck, the Minor Pentatonic scale in C looks like this:

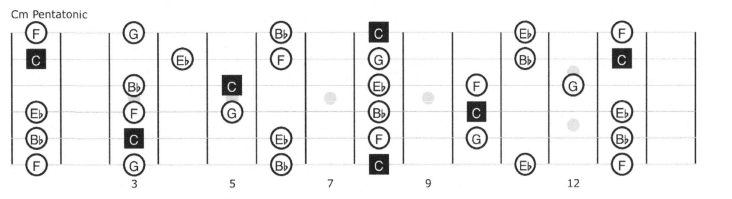

The Minor Pentatonic scale does not contain a 2nd or a 6th: its formula is 1 b3 4 5 b7.

As Minor Pentatonic scales don't have seven notes, triad and arpeggio structures are unusual. However, they are well suited to melodic sequences and intervallic approaches, albeit with a somewhat reduced range of possibilities.

The following ideas are the most useful scale sequence and interval ideas to explore with the Minor Pentatonic scale. They are all written as even 1/8th notes, but you should also experiment by playing them as triplets to create 4 against 3 feels as you learnt in previous chapters.

Begin by using the following ideas with just the first position of the C Minor Pentatonic scale before applying them to the four other shapes. The following schedule will help you to organise your practice:

Pattern	Day 1	Day 2	Day 3	Day 4	Day 5	Day 6	Day 7
A*	♪@60	♪@80	♪@100	♫@50	♫@75	♫@90	♫@100
B*	♪@60	♪@80	♪@100	♫@50	♫@75	♫@90	♫@100
C	♪@60	♪@80	♪@100	♫@50	♫@75	♫@90	♫@100
D*	♪@60	♪@80	♪@100	♫@50	♫@75	♫@90	♫@100
E*	♪@60	♪@80	♪@100	♫@50	♫@75	♫@90	♫@100
F	♪@60	♪@80	♪@100	♫@50	♫@75	♫@90	♫@100
G*	♪³@60	♪³@80	♪³@100	♫⁶@50	♫⁶@60	♫⁶@70	♫⁶@80
H	♪³@60	♪³@80	♪³@100	♫⁶@50	♫⁶@60	♫⁶@70	♫⁶@80
I*	♪³@60	♪³@80	♪³@100	♫⁶@50	♫⁶@60	♫⁶@70	♫⁶@80
J*	♪@60	♪@80	♪@100	♫@50	♫@75	♫@90	♫@100
K*	♪@60	♪@80	♪@100	♫@50	♫@75	♫@90	♫@100

Example 6a: (ascending) *

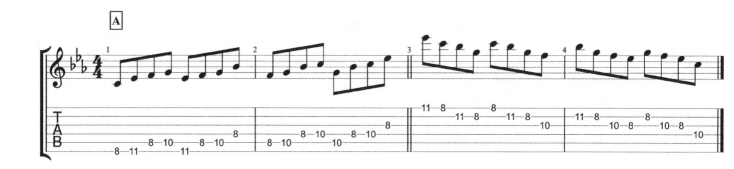

Example 6b: (descending) *

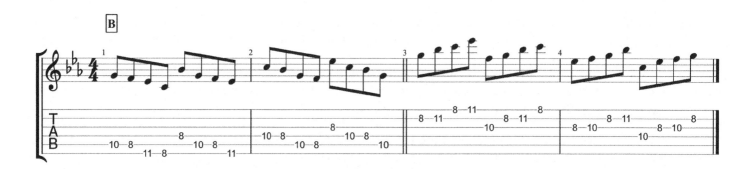

Example 6c: (three up)

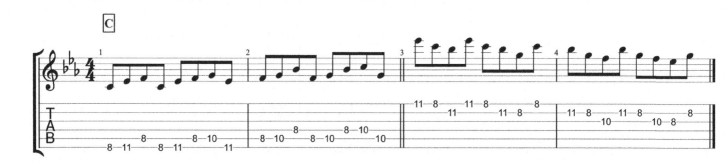

Example 6d: (rock pattern)

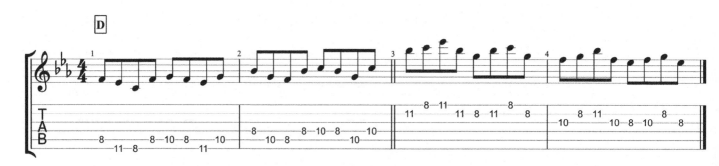

Example 6e: (rock pattern 2) *

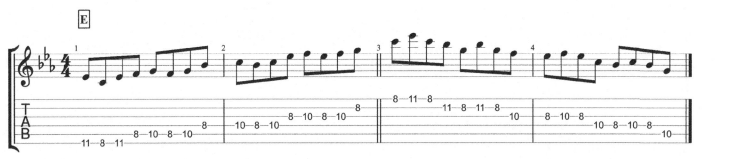

Example 6f: (in out)

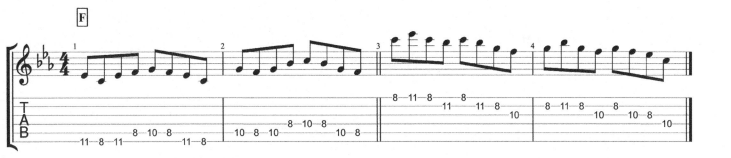

Example 6g: (triplets) *

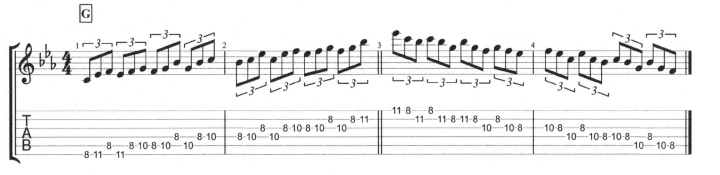

Example 6h: (in out)

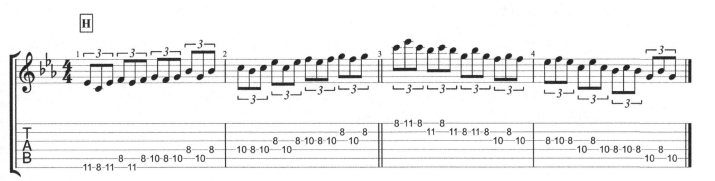

Example 6i: (4 against 3) *

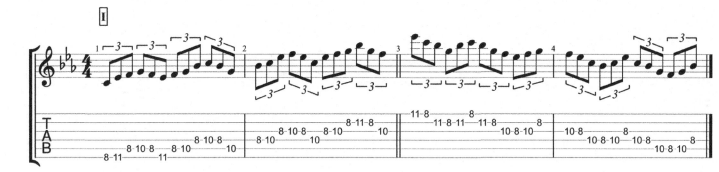

Example 6j: (4ths) *

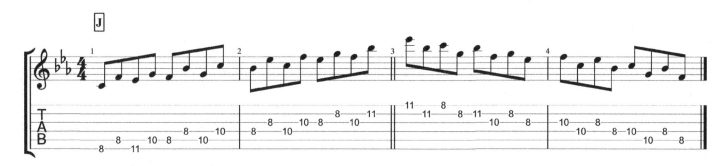

Example 6k: (ascend then descend in 4ths) *

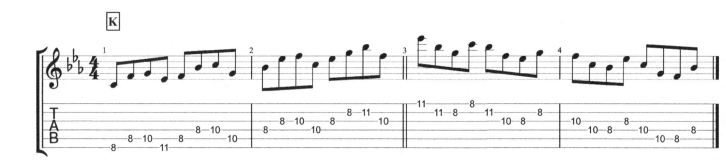

Don't forget to get creative with the Minor Pentatonic ideas using the approaches in Chapter Five.

Melodic Minor Scale Shapes

All the sequence, interval, triad, and arpeggio patterns you have learnt with the Major scale shapes can be applied to the Melodic and Harmonic Minor scales.

To illustrate this, I will show you how to apply one sequence, one interval, one triad, and one arpeggio pattern from the earlier chapters to shape 1 of the Melodic Minor scale.

Begin by learning to play the first shape of the Melodic Minor scale:

Example 6l:

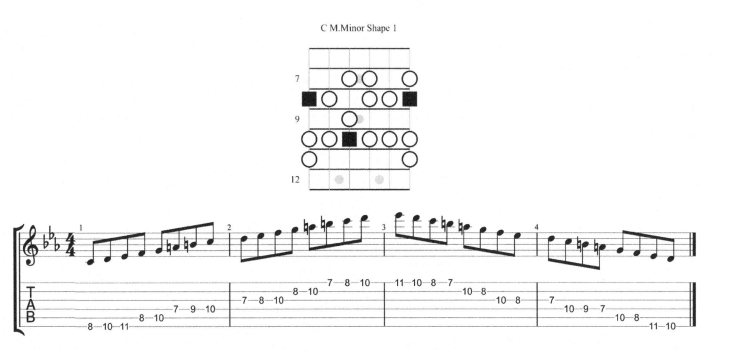

Let's apply the sequence pattern from example 1a to the Melodic Minor scale. To refresh your memory, the sequence on the Major scale was this:

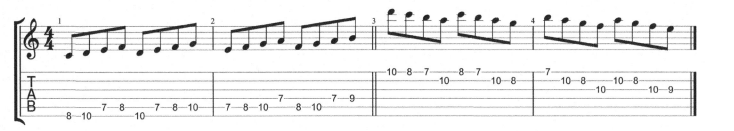

If we apply the same sequence shape to the Melodic Minor scale we get:

Example 6m:

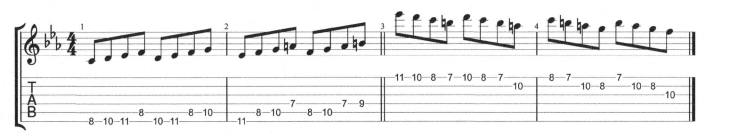

As you can see and hear, the sequence of four ascending notes is the same in both examples, but the actual notes are different because of the different scale construction. The following examples show how to use the initial interval, triad and arpeggio sequence from the earlier chapters with the Melodic Minor scale.

Example 6n: (thirds in Melodic Minor shape 1)

Example 6o: (triads in Melodic Minor shape 1)

Example 6p: (arpeggios in Melodic Minor shape 1)

The fingering for the Melodic Minor scale is a little more challenging than the Major scale, but it can help to remember that these two scales are almost identical. C Melodic Minor is simply a C Major scale with a b3.

C Major Formula: 1 2 3 4 5 6 7

C Melodic Minor Formula 1 2 b3 4 5 6 7

It can help to view Melodic Minor as an adjusted Major scale if you're having trouble remembering the scale shapes.

Apply the rest of the patterns from each of these chapters yourself using the practice schedules to help you organise your approach. Begin by applying the melodic structures to shape 1 of the Melodic Minor scale, but as you gain confidence, learn the other four scale shapes and apply the structures to each shape in turn. These are shown on the following page.

It helps to learn the following Melodic Minor scale shapes around the chord 'anchors' shown in black in the following diagrams. You will learn much more about this concept in Part Two.

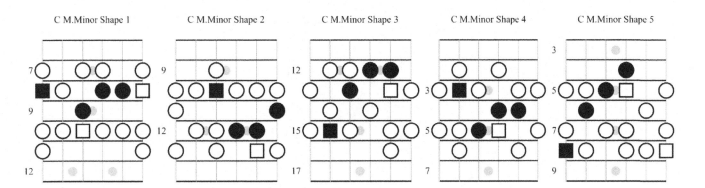

Use the practice schedules from earlier chapters to help you organise your approach.

Harmonic Minor Scale Shapes

As with the Melodic Minor scale, all the patterns from the earlier chapters can be applied to the Harmonic Minor scale.

Shape 1 of the C Harmonic Minor scale can be played as follows:

Example 6q:

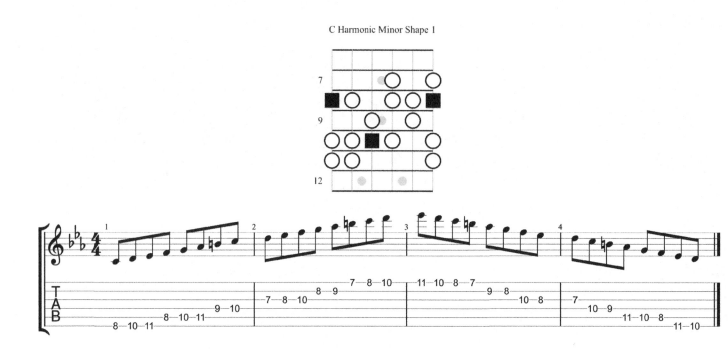

As with the Melodic Minor scale, I will show you how to apply only the first ideas from Chapters One, Two and Three to the Harmonic Minor scale.

Example 6r: (sequence in Harmonic Minor shape 1)

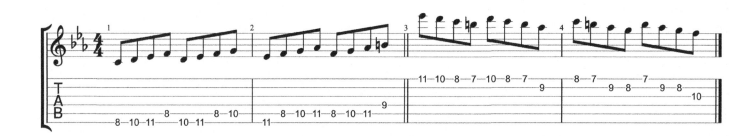

Example 6s: (thirds in Harmonic Minor shape 1)

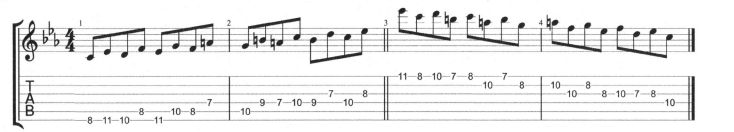

Example 6t: (triads in Harmonic Minor shape 1)

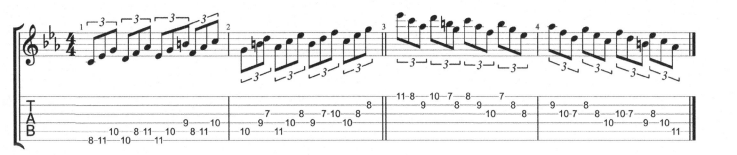

Example 6u: (arpeggios in Harmonic Minor shape 1)

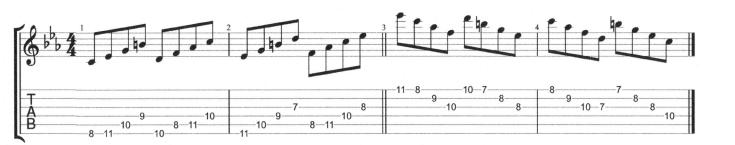

As you gain confidence with the shape 1 Harmonic Minor patterns, apply the ideas to the other four shapes of the Harmonic Minor scale.

It will help to learn the Harmonic Minor scale shapes around the chord 'anchors' shown in black in the following diagrams. You will learn more about this in Part Two.

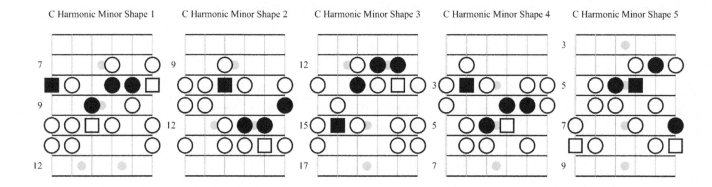

Use the practice schedules from earlier chapters to help you organise your approach.

This section of the book may seem quite short, but applying all the sequences to all the scale shapes will take many weeks. There is no hurry to master everything, so make sure you combine these ideas with other creative, musical areas, and the CAGED system approach in Part Two.

I would suggest spending only about 20 minutes each day on the patterns in this chapter. Remember that real musical benefit comes from applying these ideas, not just learning them.

Chapter Seven: Two-Octave Arpeggios

In Chapter Four, each scale was broken into four-note arpeggio fragments beginning on each step of the scale. Each of the arpeggios built on scale steps can also be isolated and their notes played over two octaves.

There are many possible arpeggios in music, but the four most common ones are the Major 7, Minor 7, Dominant 7 and Min7b5 (or 'half diminished') arpeggios. As these arpeggio types are all four-note structures, we can once again learn melodic patterns around one arpeggio and then apply those patterns to the other three arpeggio types.

As with scales, there are five shapes for each arpeggio although you will gain most benefit by focusing on shape 1 and using those ideas to make music, before moving on to the other four shapes of each arpeggio type.

Begin by learning these useful melodic patterns around shape 1 of the C Major 7 arpeggio before applying these patterns to the other four Major 7 arpeggio shapes and then to the other arpeggio types.

The shape 1 Major 7 arpeggio is played in the following way:

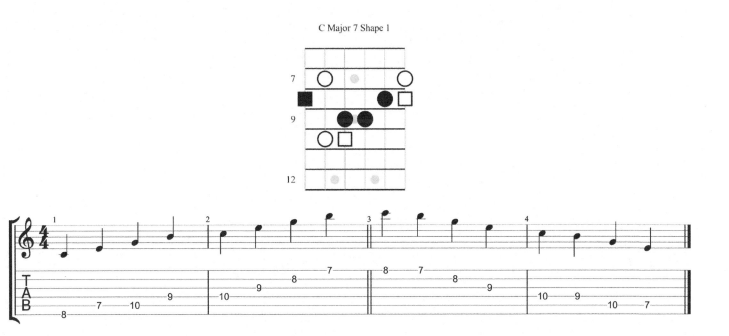

Notice that this example consists of *only* the first four notes of Example 4a. However, instead of starting a new four-note arpeggio on the second note of the scale (D), the four notes are repeated in a higher octave.

Many melodic sequences can be built by varying the order of just these four notes. Two-octave arpeggio patterns can be technically challenging but they really alert your ears to some exciting musical ideas while developing excellent vision and fluency on the guitar.

The following sequences are the most useful ones to begin with when mastering four-note arpeggios in two octaves.

Example 7a: *

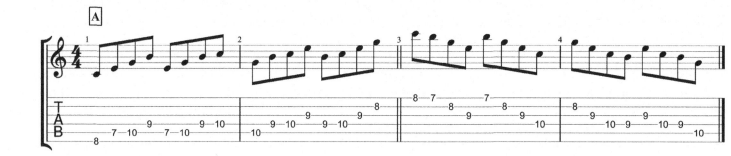

Example 7b: *

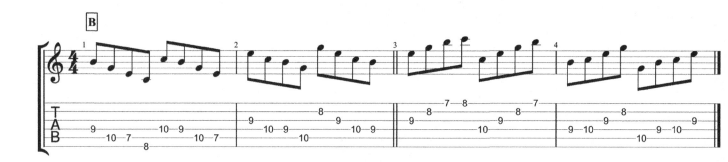

Example 7c: *

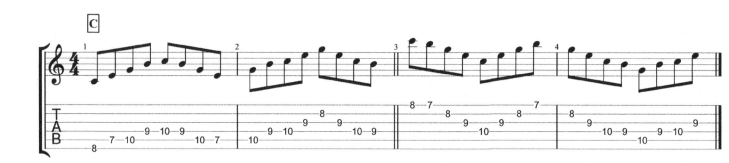

Example 7d:

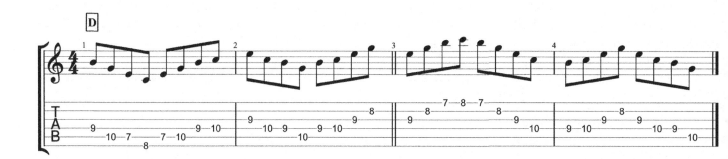

Example 7e:

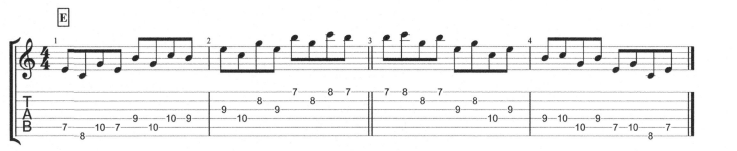

Example 7f:

Example 7g:

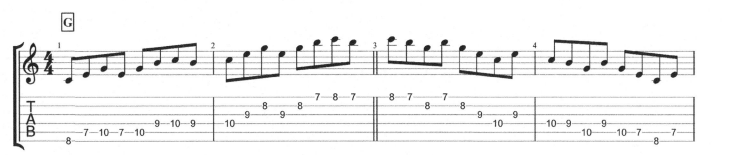

Example 7h:

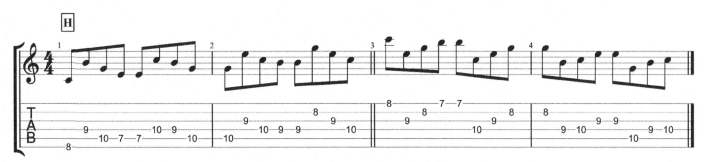

Apply these melodic patterns to shape 1 of each arpeggio type (Major 7, Minor 7, Dominant 7 and Min7b5).

This is how Example 7a would be played with shape 1 of a C Dominant 7 arpeggio:

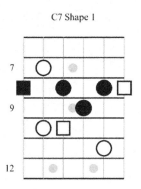

C7 Shape 1

Example 7i:

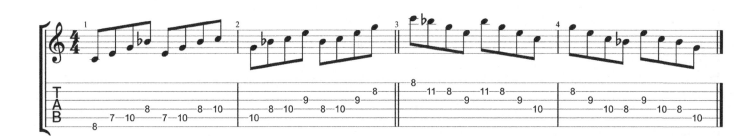

Try using the melodic patterns in examples 7a – 7h with the C7 arpeggio above before learning them with shape 1 of the Minor 7 (m7) and then Minor 7b5 (m7b5) arpeggios below:

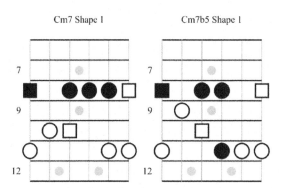

Cm7 Shape 1   Cm7b5 Shape 1

As you begin to hear how these arpeggios sound and develop confidence with shape 1 of each arpeggio, add the other four shapes of each arpeggio into your practice routine. Start by memorising each arpeggio shape ascending and descending, and only tackle one arpeggio quality each week. For example, in week one, work on all five shapes of Major 7, then in week two work on all five shapes of m7, etc.

You do not need to neglect your previous week's study as it should only take a few minutes to recap the other arpeggio patterns at the end of your practice routine.

The five shapes for each arpeggio type are shown below. Practice them with their backing tracks to get a feel for how these sounds work in a musical context.

Major 7 Arpeggios (backing track three)

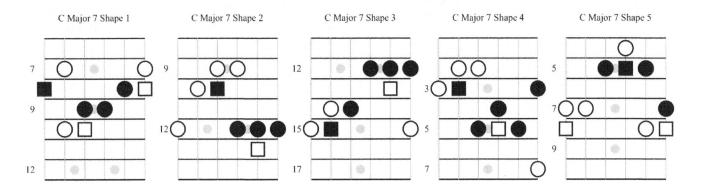

Dominant 7 Arpeggios (backing track four)

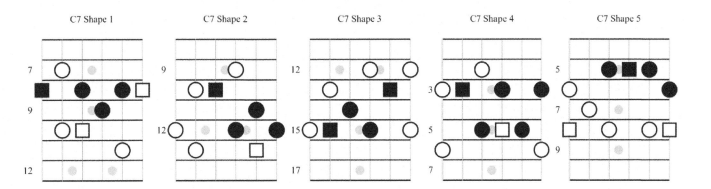

Minor 7 Arpeggios (backing track five)

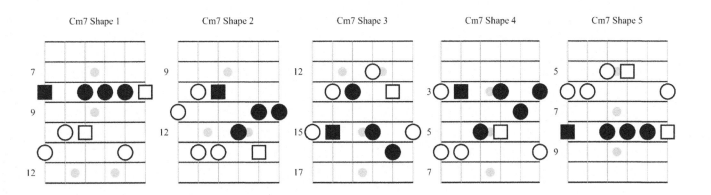

m7b5 Arpeggios (backing track six)

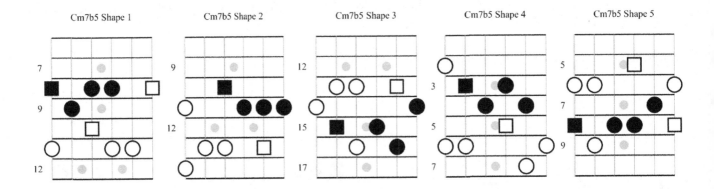

Chapter Eight: Two-Octave Triads

Just as with four-note arpeggios, three-note triads can be studied in isolation. There are four types of triad: Major, Minor, Diminished and Augmented. While Diminished and Augmented triads are occasionally used, Major and Minor triads are the most common approaches so we will focus exclusively on these to begin with.

The following melodic patterns are shown in the first position of C Major. Learn them in this position before applying them to the other triad types in five positions.

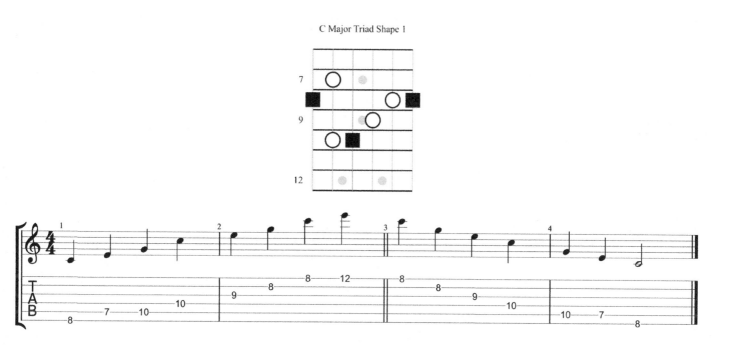

Example 8a:

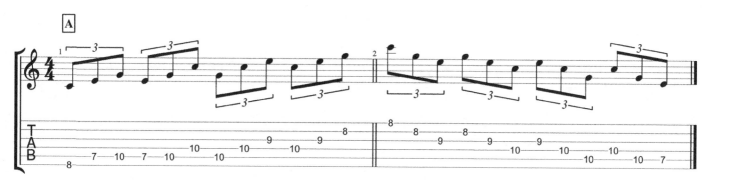

Example 8b:

Example 8c:

Example 8d:

Example 8e:

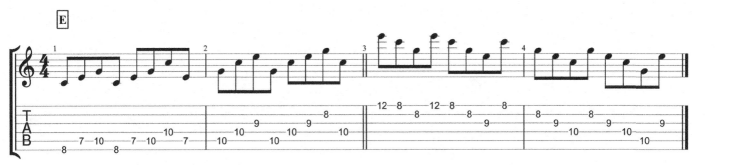

The four types of triad can be played in five positions in the following way:

Major Triads

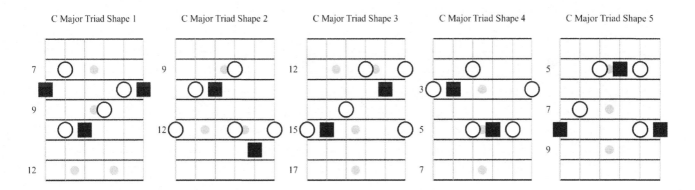

Minor Triads

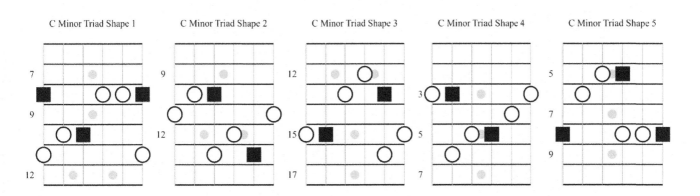

Diminished Triads

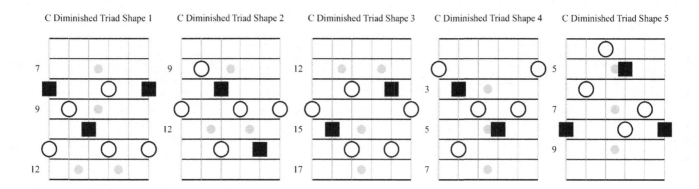

Augmented Triads

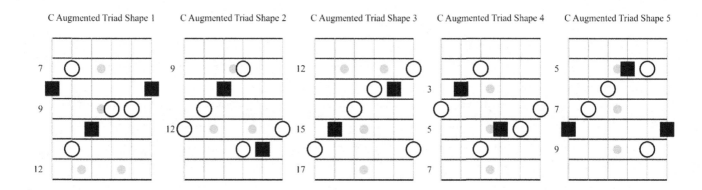

Part Two: Scales, Positions and Keys

Introduction to Part Two

In this section you will learn to play every common scale or mode in any key, anywhere on the neck using a simple method called the CAGED system.

The CAGED system works by assigning an-easy-to-remember chord 'anchor' to each scale shape, enabling you to quickly visualise the scale or mode built around it. The chord anchor also outlines the mood of each mode so that when you play the chord, you can hear the fundamental musical qualities of each scale. For example, we build the Major scale around a Major chord, but we build the Dorian mode around a Minor 7 chord.

We can use the same five Major scale shapes you have been working with so far to play *any* mode. The only things to change are the chord which we visualise the scale around and when it is used musically.

The guitar neck is organised into five different positions and there are five different shapes for each parent scale. To allow us to apply the five shapes of each scale in all five positions of the neck, we practice exercises in five different keys: one key per shape.

By using five different keys we can 'lock' the fretting hand into one area of the guitar and use each of the five shapes to play the scale in a different key. This is a fantastic way to learn and internalise any scale and to do some mental gymnastics!

This may seem confusing at first but don't worry. You will slowly be taken through this process step by step. Once you have learnt this process with one scale in one position of the guitar, it is relatively simple to transfer this process to any scale, in any position on the neck. As you become more familiar with the notes on the neck, it becomes easy to move the anchor chord to another key, and instantly build the correct scale, mode or lick around it.

This method is much easier when you know the notes on the bottom three strings of the guitar, so spend time working through the following three pages before you launch into Chapter Ten. Everything you need is recapped in each section, but putting some work in here will ease the journey.

Chapter Nine: Fretboard Recognition

To be able to play a scale in any key, it is essential to know where the root notes of that scale lie on the guitar neck. The system in this book only requires you to know the notes on the three bass strings but I strongly urge you to learn the whole neck fluently. The notes you need will be recapped in the next section but working through this chapter will be an excellent primer for what comes later.

Let's look at some extremely useful patterns that help us quickly determine the name and location of *any* note on the guitar neck.

The first thing to learn is the location of notes on the 6th and 5th strings:

Notes on the 6th string:

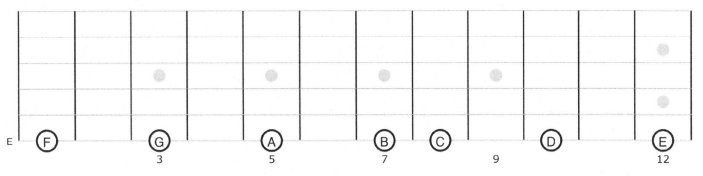

Notes on the 6th String

Notes on the 5th string:

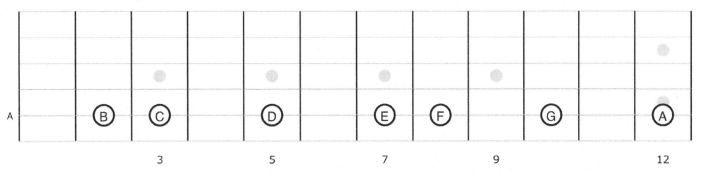

Notes on the 5th String

If you already use barre chords, you may be familiar with the locations of these notes.

Remember, each note can be adjusted to become a sharp (#) or a flat (b) by shifting it up or down a semitone. For example, Eb and D# are both located on the 5th string, 6th fret or the 6th string, 11th fret.

Octave patterns are consistent shapes that show us how to locate notes of the same name on the guitar.

We can use these simple shapes to find the any note in a higher octave.

Octaves are played between the 6th and 4th strings or between the 5th and 3rd strings in the following way:

Octave Pattern 6th to 4th String and 5th to 3rd String

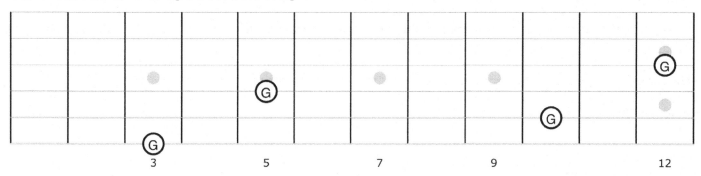

To play the same note an octave higher you always move *across* two strings and *up* two frets.

Using this information, you can quickly figure out all the notes on the 4th and 3rd strings.

You can also play an octave by skipping *two* strings. Here is the octave pattern between the 6th and 3rd strings:

Octave Pattern 6th to 3rd String

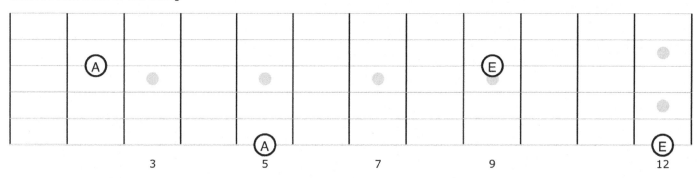

If you know the note on the 6th string, you can locate the same note an octave higher on the 3rd string by moving *across* three strings and *down* three frets.

There is a similar, but slightly different pattern between the 5th and 2nd strings. Because of the tuning idiosyncrasy between the 3rd and 2nd strings on the guitar, the pattern alters slightly:

Octave Pattern 5th to 2nd String

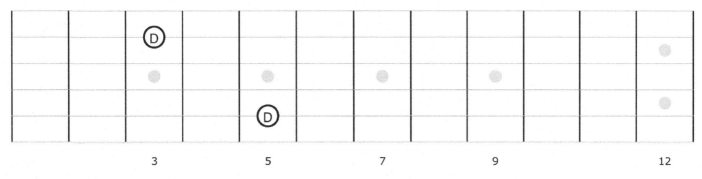

If you know the name of a note on the 5th string, you can locate the same note an octave higher on the 2nd string by moving *across* three strings and *down* two frets.

Between the 4th and 2nd strings, an octave shape will always look like this:

Octave Pattern 4th to 2nd String

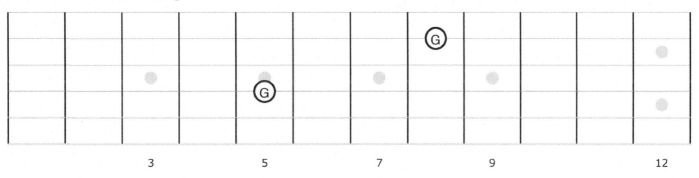

This is identical to the octave pattern between the 3rd and 1st strings:

Octave Pattern 3rd to 1st String

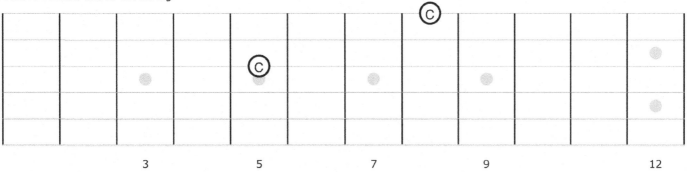

Finally, you may already know that the notes on the 1st string are identical to the notes on the 6th string, just two octaves higher:

Two Octave Pattern

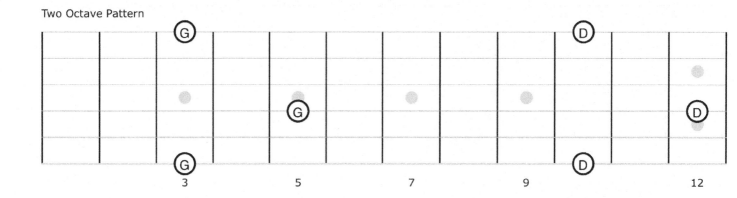

An essential part of learning the neck is developing *instant* recall of these patterns. With practice, the neck seems to get smaller and it takes less and less time to play a phrase.

A fun game is to say a note name out loud and then quickly try to find *every* possible location of that note on the neck. Don't forget to try it with sharp and flat notes too.

In the following chapters, you will be doing a lot of *positional* practice in the keys of A, C, D, F and G, and knowing the locations of these notes is essential.

Chapter Ten: The CAGED System with the Major Scale

In Part One we worked only in the key of C, and learnt the five positions of the C Major scale in the following way:

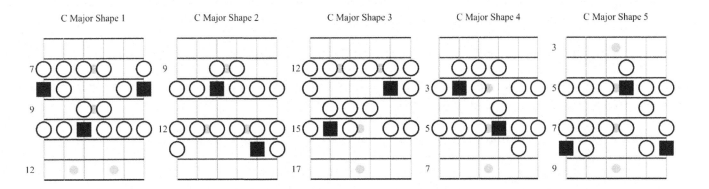

We were concerned only with where the root note (C) lay on the guitar to play in the correct key.

In Part Two, we will learn to play any of these shapes instantly in any key, anywhere on the neck. For example, if you want to play an A Major scale between the second and fifth frets, how would you know which scale shape to use?

First, we need to know where the root note (A) is in that location.

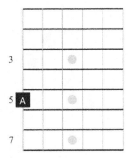

We then need to find the shape of the Major scale that aligns with the root note, while keeping our hand in this position. With a little investigation of the above patterns, you might see that this is shape 5:

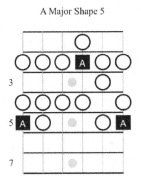

A Major Shape 5

We have transposed (shifted) position 5 of the C Major scale down the neck so that the new root note is A. This is the same process as moving a barre chord around on the neck.

This procedure is a little slow and requires us to think about many different things. When you multiply this process by every scale and mode in all twelve keys, you get an idea of the complexity that could become involved. Musicians tend not to think like this because this slow, step-by-step process gets in the way of creativity and spontaneity.

We don't want to be worrying about how to locate scale notes; we simply want to make music.

The answer to this problem is to develop a quick system that works with any scale, in any key, anywhere on the neck. To use this system, you only need to:

- Know where the root notes are on the neck (at least on the bottom three strings)

- Learn the scale shape around an easy to remember barre chord

By moving barre chords up and down the neck we can access any chord. By linking these bar chord shapes to scales, we can access any scale.

Another advantage of this system is that the barre chord shapes help to define the sound and feel of each mode and help us link musical ideas and licks to these chords. For example, the Dorian mode is normally played over 'chilled out' Minor 7 chords, so we learn Dorian with Minor 7 barre chords as anchors. By doing this, we train our ears to link the sound of the chord with the mood of the scale.

To get started, let's look at the Major scale shapes again, but this time let's build them around Major barre chords.

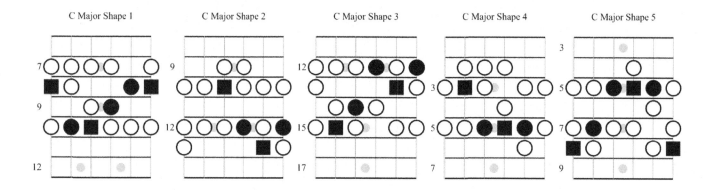

The hollow markers show the scale notes and the solid markers show different barre chord shapes of the C Major chord. You will see that these chord shapes are barre chord versions of some of the first chords you will have learnt on the guitar, E, D, C, A and G. Rearranging these notes gives rise to the name 'The CAGED System'.

To memorise the scale shapes in conjunction with the chords:

- Play the barre chord anchor and say the name of the chord out loud

- Ascend and descend through the scale shape

- Play the barre chord anchor and say the name of the scale out loud

- Repeat these steps but play the scale from the highest note and descend then ascend

- Finally, visualise (but don't play) the chord shape as you play through the scale ascending and descending, then descending and ascending

Occasionally it is easier *not* to play every note in every anchor chord (e.g., positions 2 and 5), but make sure you strongly visualise the root of each chord shape, especially in position 5 when it is possible for it to be omitted.

Example 10a: (Backing track three**)**

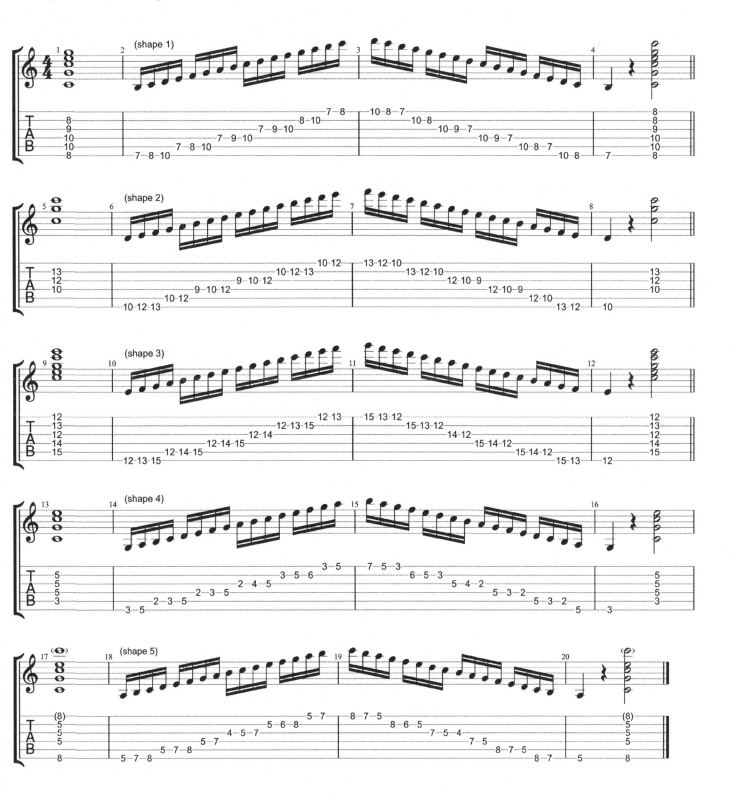

Repeat this exercise first descending then ascending each scale after playing each chord anchor.

Now try linking each scale position together from low to high as shown.

Example 10b:

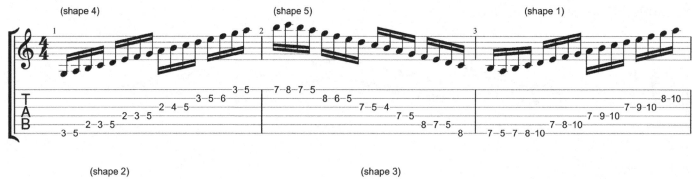

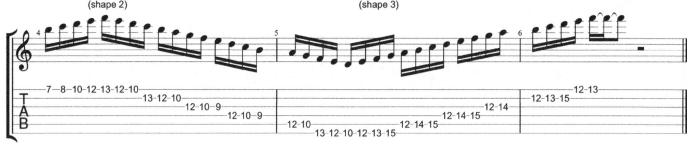

Be careful to follow the tablature locations and change between the five positions at the right time.

You can also play Example 10b backwards and descend the neck. Learn to do this without looking at the notation.

The next stage is to learn to use all five scale shapes to play the Major scale in *different keys* in the same position on the neck. The idea is to use one of the five Major scale shapes for each key and to play through five different keys.

The key centres that we will use for this exercise are A, C, D, F and G Major. These keys can all be played in one position on the neck using the five Major scale shapes. We always play through the key centres in the order A, C, D, F and then G.

The first thing to do is to learn where the root note of each key lies on the neck. We will begin in the middle of the guitar neck between the 5th and 8th frets.

The notes A, C, D, F and G are here on the fretboard:

5th to 8th fret

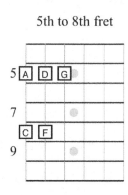

Which Major scale shape do we need to use to play the scale of A Major in this position? Flip back to see which scale diagram contains a barre chord shape that easily aligns with the note A in the above diagram.

Can you see that shape 1 contains a Major barre chord shape that will line up with the A root note? Here is the shape 1 Major scale shape in the key of A:

A Major (Shape 1)

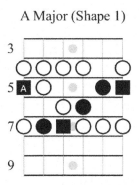

Play the A Major barre chord and then play up and down the A Major scale. Start on the lowest note of the shape, not the root note.

Example 10c:

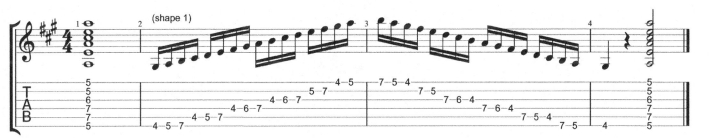

The next key in the sequence is C Major.

The note C is located on the 8th fret on the 6th string. Which barre chord shape aligns its root with the note C?

If you look carefully, you will see that *shape 5* is the only possible chord that has a root in the right place when your hand is locked in the 5th to 8th fret area of the guitar.

C Major (Shape 5)

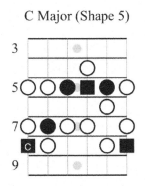

Play the C Major barre chord and then play up and down through the scale beginning on the lowest note.

Example 10d:

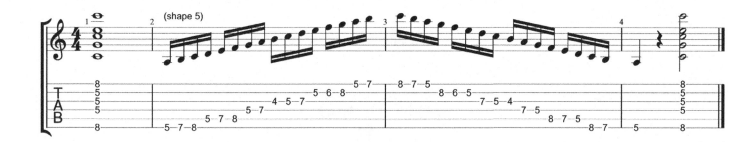

The next key in the sequence is D Major. The note D is located on the 5th fret of the 5th string. You would use shape 4 to play the scale of D Major in this position.

D Major (Shape 4)

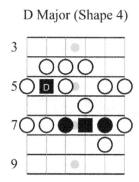

Play the D Major barre chord and then play up and down through the scale.

Example 10e:

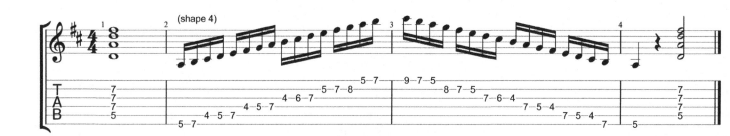

Next in the sequence of key centres is F Major. In this position, the scale of F Major is played with shape 3.

F Major (Shape 3)

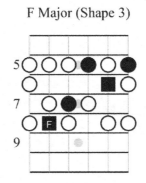

Repeat the process of playing chord – scale – chord.

Example 10f:

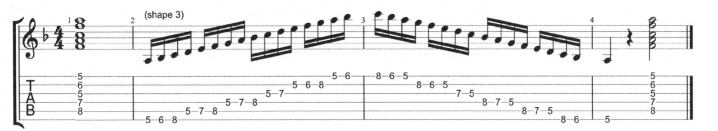

The final key centre in the sequence is G Major. The root of G is a little trickier to see as it is on the 4th string. In this position you access the G Major scale by using Shape 2.

G Major (Shape 2)

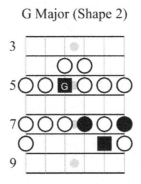

Example 10g:

Try closing the book and playing the scales of A, C, D, F and G Major in turn from memory. Begin by playing the anchor chord and then ascend and descend each Major scale shape.

Example 10h: (Backing track seven)

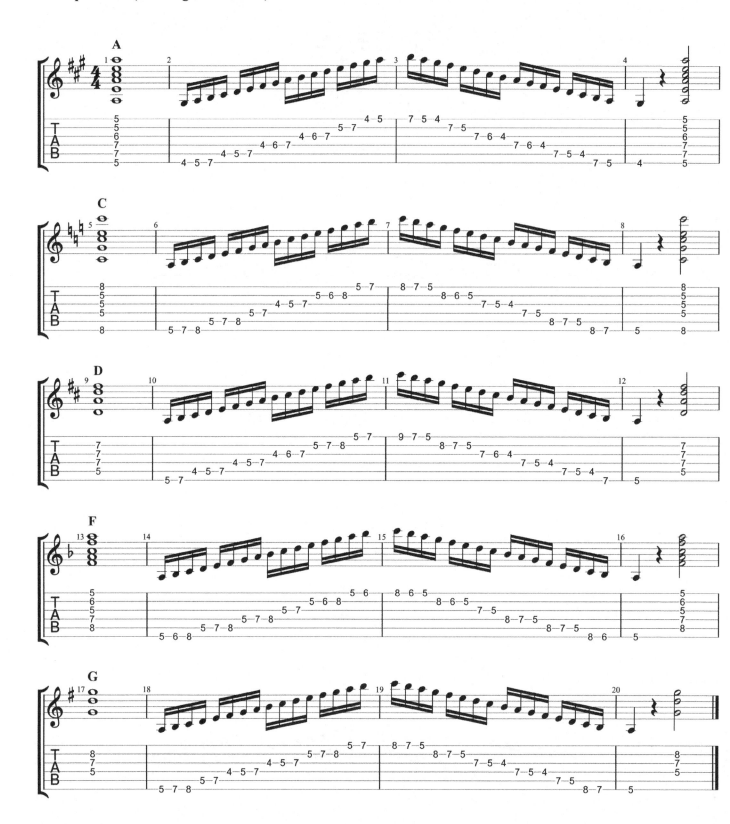

The next stage is to run through the Major scale key centres of A, C, D, F and G again, but this time do *not* play the chords.

Visualise the chords in your mind and say each scale name out loud as you play it.

Example 10i: (Backing track eight)

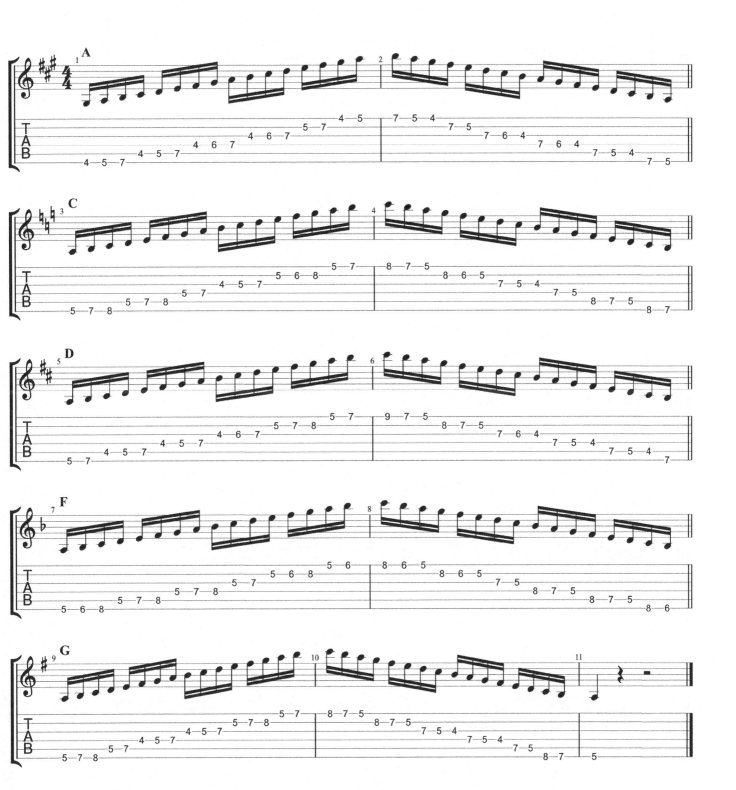

Finally, ascend one shape and then descend the next.

Example 10j: (Backing track nine)

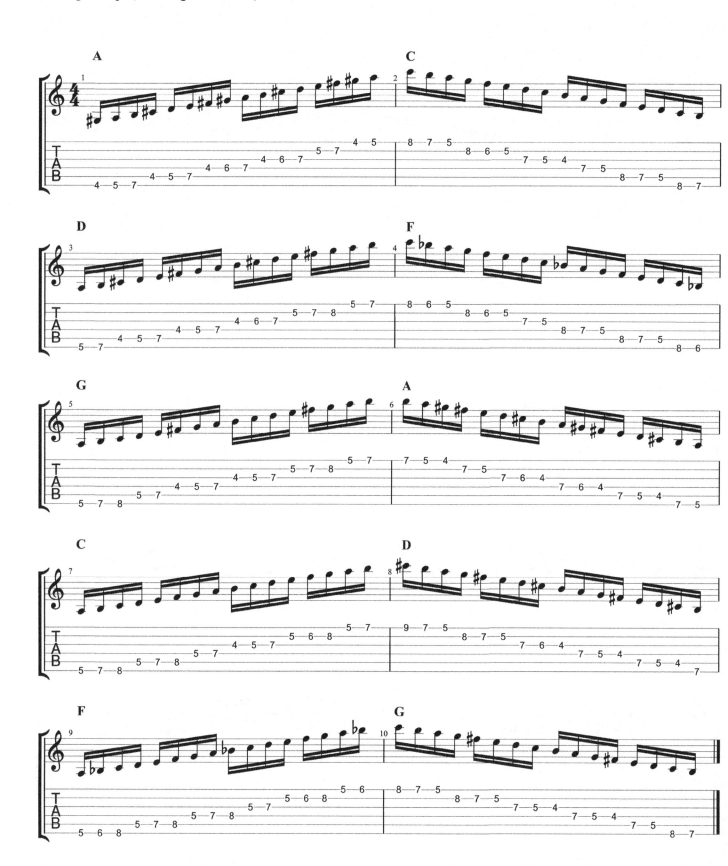

Chapter Eleven: All Neck Positions

We have covered the five positions of the Major scale and created strong mental links between the anchor chord and the scale shape. Now it is time to open up the neck by moving the ACDFG exercise into different positions.

If you've done the hard work in the previous chapter, this section should be relatively straightforward. When students struggle, it's normally due to not knowing where the root notes are on the guitar neck. Once you can easily locate the root notes, the process is simple:

- Find the root note

- Align the root of the correct chord shape with the root note

- Visualise and play the scale

Let's move up the neck into a different position and play through the ACDFG in the 7th to 10th fret area. Here are the root notes of each scale:

7th to 10th fret

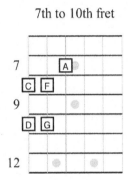

In this position, the note A is on the 4th string. You should quickly be able to see that this position aligns with shape 2 of the Major scale:

A Major (Shape 2)

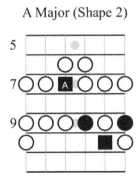

Repeat the process used in the previous chapter. Play the anchor chord, ascend and descend the scale from the lowest to the highest note and then play the anchor chord again.

Repeat this process for the remaining keys individually, before joining up the five key centres as before.

To get you started, here are the scale diagrams for the five keys in this position. Make sure you understand that each scale shape has an associated chord anchor that needs to be aligned with the root note of the key you want to play.

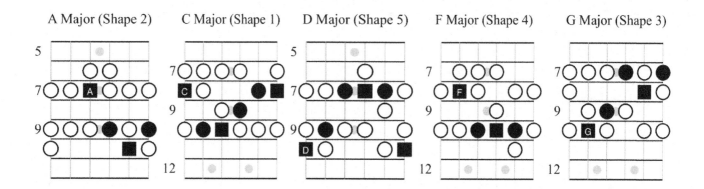

Play through the following exercises using the scale shapes in the 7th to 10th fret positions.

In the order A, C, D, F and then G Major

- Play the chord, ascend and descend the scale, play the chord. Say the chord names out loud

- Play the chord, descend then ascend the scale, play the chord. Say the chord names out loud

- *Visualise* the chord, ascend and descend each scale

- *Visualise* the chord, descend then ascend each scale

- Ascend one shape then descend the next, e.g., ascend A Major, descend C Major, etc.

- Descend one shape then ascend the next, e.g., descend A Major, ascend C Major, etc.

Work with a metronome to ensure your rhythm is consistent (especially when changing chords) before gradually increasing your speed.

You will find that it takes you less and less time to use these shapes in new positions. As soon as you are comfortable with the locations of the root notes on the neck you will be able to quickly see the appropriate chord and instantly build the scale around it.

Every few days, try the above ACDFG exercises in a new position on the fretboard. There are five positions on the neck and the root notes are located as follows.

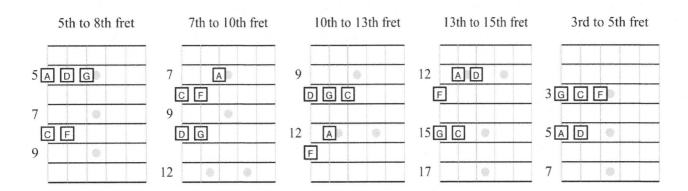

It may take you a little while to work through all five positions on the neck, but soon you will be able to quickly run through every scale in every key each day. Eventually you will be able to run through all five keys in all five positions in under two minutes (1/16th notes at 90 bpm).

The final stage in the process (after you have become confident in all five positions on the neck) is to be able to work in *any* key. We have covered five of the most common keys with the ACDFG sequence, but there are 12 keys in music.

All we need to know is where the desired root note is on the neck and then place the correct anchor chord there. Here are the notes on the bottom three strings of the guitar.

Notes on the Bass Strings

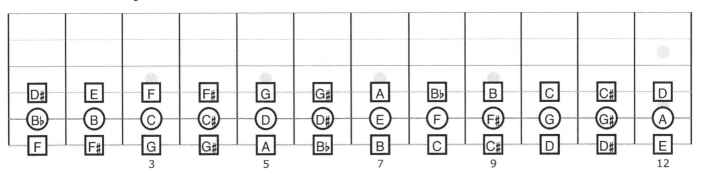

Test yourself! Answers below.

1. Which chord/scale shape would you use if you wanted to play B Major at the 2nd fret?

2. Which chord/scale shape would you use if you wanted to play Bb Major at the 6th to 8th fret?

3. Which chord/scale shape would you use if you wanted to play E Major and your hand was located between the 5th and 7th frets?

---

1 **1)** Shape 4. **2)** Shape 1. **3)** Shape 3. **4)** Shape 4. **5)** Shape 2. **6)** Shape 5.

4. Which chord/scale shape would you use if you wanted to play D# Major and your hand was located between the 5th and 7th frets?

5. Which scale shape would you use to play F# Major if your hand was in the 3rd to 6th fret area?

6. Which scale shape would you use to play G# Major if your hand was in the 1st to 4th fret area?

The most important thing you can do now is to learn the notes on the bottom three strings. Flick back to Chapter Nine to help you.

Chapter Twelve: Application to Other Scales

All the other modes can be mastered by using chord anchors just as with the Major scale. We use the same five scale shapes as before to play each of the seven Major modes, and to do this we simply view each shape around a different anchor chord.

If you are struggling with the concept of building modes, then you should check out my book **The Practical Guide to Modern Music Theory for Guitarists**.

The Dorian mode is normally played over a m7 groove and it creates a laidback, jazzy vibe. Dorian is the second mode of the Major scale and its interval formula is 1 2 b3 4 5 6 b7. It is important to know that the Dorian mode is created by starting on the second note of a Major scale and playing through all the notes of the Major scale in sequence.

For example, if the 'parent' Major scale is C Major (C D E F G A B C), the Dorian mode would start on the second note of the scale (D) and contain all of the notes of C Major (D E F G A B C D).

While a mode like Dorian is *derived* from a parent scale, musicians rarely refer back to this parent. Instead, we see the Dorian mode as a separate scale with its own identity, harmony and mood. It is simply a coincidence that it happens to contain the same notes as a different Major scale.

If you play the notes D E F G A B C D on your guitar, there is a fair chance you will still hear it as a C Major scale because most popular and classical music has been created using Major scales for hundreds of years. You've been 'trained' to hear these notes resolving to the root of the Major scale (in this case C) all your life.

Using modes is all about context and this can be seen in the following two examples.

In the first example, the notes of D Dorian are played descending over a C Major chord groove. You will hear the sequence of notes wanting to resolve down to the tonic of the chord (C).

In the second example, you will hear the same notes played over a Dm7 chord groove. This time you will hear that the notes want to resolve to the tonic of D.

The mood of the music is very different between these two examples.

Example 12a:

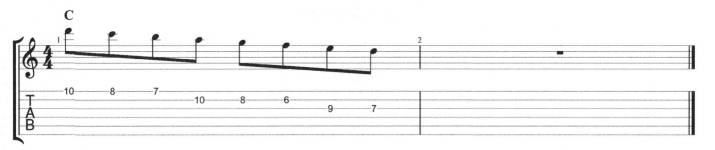

Example 12b:

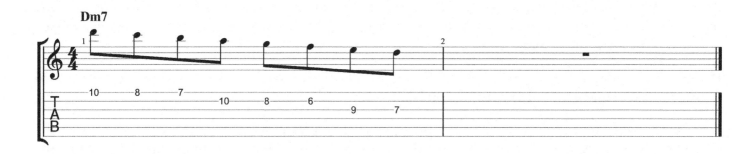

Modes are a big subject and this book assumes you have some experience and understanding of their use. If you have any questions, please check out **Guitar Scales in Context** and **The Practical Guide to Modern Music Theory for Guitarists** for in-depth tuition on all the modes and how they're used.

As you could hear in the previous two examples, the way we perceive the same set of notes depends on the context in which they're heard. The same notes can have a very different mood when they're heard over different chords, even in the simple examples above.

The most useful thing when learning scales is to learn them in context. This is why it's important to associate them with a chord anchor. The anchor isn't just there to help you remember the shape of the scale, it is there to help you hear and feel the mood of the scale.

Let's look now at how we can use the chord anchor approach to learn the Dorian mode.

Dorian is a Minor mode because it contains a minor 3rd, or 'b3'. This can be seen in its scale formula (1 2 b3 4 5 6 b7). The chord formed when the tonic (root) note is harmonised is a Minor 7 (1 b3 5 b7). Using this Minor 7 (m7) chord as our anchor allows us to hear the Dorian mode in context.

Shape 1 of the Dorian mode in C can be played in the following way:

C Dorian Shape 1

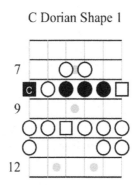

You will recognise this scale shape from earlier but as I mentioned before, do not think of it as the second shape of the Major scale, see it as Dorian shape 1. It has a completely new identity, sound and feel.

As you did with the Major scale shapes in the previous chapters, learn the Dorian mode by playing the anchor chord before ascending and descending through the scale.

Example 12c: (C Dorian shape 1)

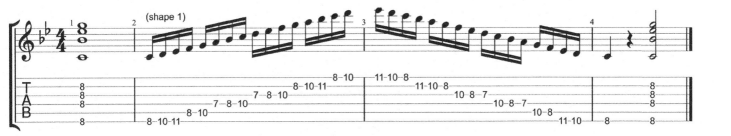

Now, take each shape in turn and learn them around their chord anchors in the key of C. You can use backing track five to help you do this.

Example 12d: (C Dorian shape 2)

C Dorian Shape 2

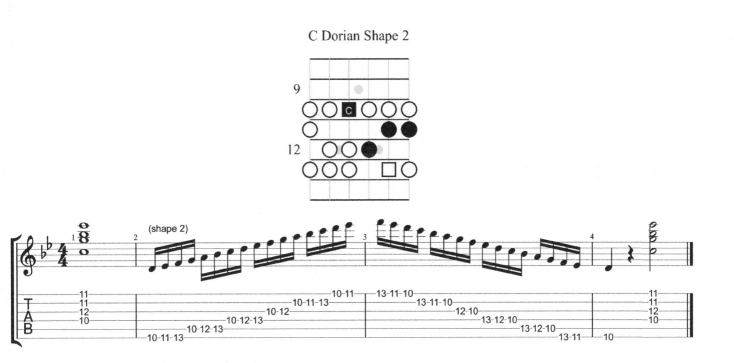

Example 12e: (C Dorian shape 3)

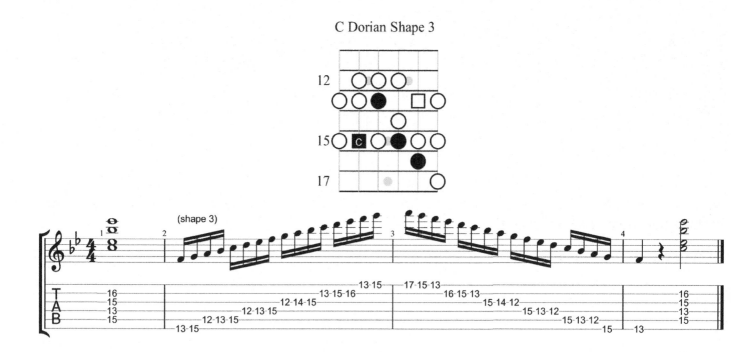

Example 12f: (C Dorian shape 4)

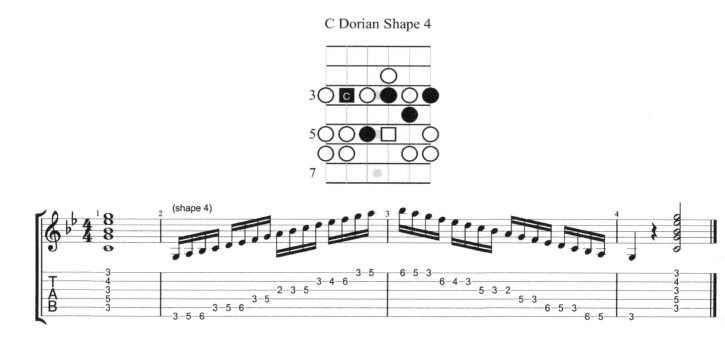

Example 12g: (C Dorian shape 5)

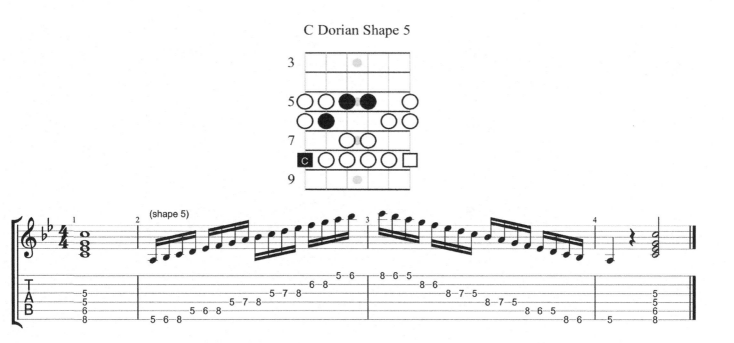

Repeat the Major scale exercises from Chapters Ten and Eleven, using the Dorian mode shapes shown above. You can practice these exercises with backing track five.

The next stage is to learn to play the Dorian mode in the keys of A, C, D, F and G in one position on the fretboard. By doing this you will quickly associate the m7 anchor chord with the Dorian scale shape and be able to open up the neck.

Remember, the process is to find the root note, play the anchor chord and finally play the scale while visualising the anchor chord.

In the 5th to 8th fret position, Dorian in the keys of A, C, D, F and G is played in the following way:

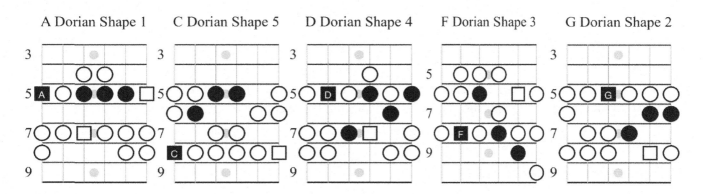

Example 12h: (with chord anchors) Backing track ten.

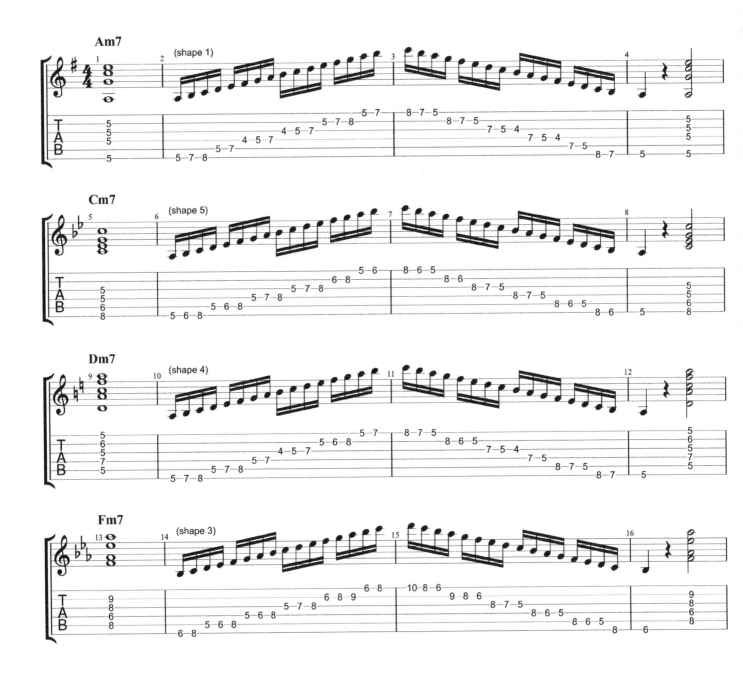

As you get better and the shapes become more internalised, repeat the exercise but omit the chords. Just visualise them as you play each scale. You can use backing track eleven to practice this.

Remember to work through the following sequence of exercises:

Play Dorian in the keys of A, C, D, F then G .

- Play the chord, ascend and descend the scale, play the chord. Say the chord names out loud

- Play the chord, descend then ascend the scale, play the chord. Say the chord names out loud

- Visualise the chord, ascend and descend each scale

- Visualise the chord, descend then ascend each scale

- Ascend one shape then descend the next, e.g., ascend A Dorian, descend C Dorian, etc. (Backing track twelve)

- Descend one shape then ascend the next, e.g., descend A Dorian, ascend C Dorian, etc.

Work with a metronome to ensure your rhythm is consistent (especially when changing chord) before gradually increasing your speed.

Every few days, try the above ACDFG exercises in a new position on the fretboard. You will be more familiar with the locations of the root notes in the other positions after having worked through Chapter Eleven.

To get you started, here are the scales of A, C, D, F and G Dorian in the 7th to 10th fret range.

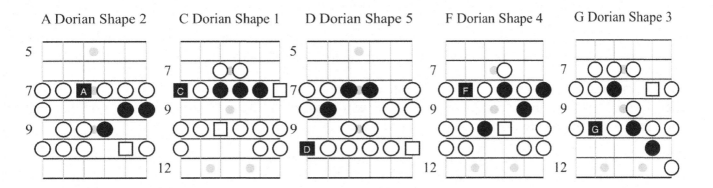

Remember, memorising these shapes simply comes down to linking the chord to the scale shape, and then placing the chord in the right place on the guitar neck to play in the desired key.

To further internalise the Dorian mode, try taking melodic sequences from Chapter One and playing them through the ACDFG exercises in each position. You can also use intervals, triads and arpeggio ideas when you get more confident. Use backing track ten to help you.

Chapter Thirteen: Why Modes Sound Different

You have seen that any mode of the Major scale can be played anywhere on the guitar by knowing just five scale shapes. The essential thing to realise is that the way we hear a set of notes (scale) depends on what chord / chord sequence is being played under it.

We will always hear the intervals of a scale in the context of the chord being played at the time. That is why in examples 12a and 12b, you heard the exact same notes functioning as different scales. The notes C D E F G A B C were heard as a scale of C Major when played over a strong C Major chord, and they were heard as D Dorian over the strong Dm7 chord.

Our ears subconsciously organise the intervals of the scale in relation to the lowest note of the chord playing at the time. Because the interval pattern of the Major scale is different to that of the Dorian mode, the two scales feel *very* different.

Without going on a massive theory digression, the Major scale has a Major 3rd (a distance of two tones) between its first and third notes (C to E). When the notes of the C Major scale are played over a strong C Major chord, our ear hears the note C as the root of the scale and organises the pitches of the scale from that point upwards. We hear the Major 3rd interval from C to E and we feel the triumphant, happy Major scale emotions.

Although the scale of D Dorian contains the same notes as C Major, we play D Dorian over a Dm or Dm7 chord. Our ear then organises the notes in context of the Dm7 chord and we hear the notes differently.

The Dorian mode has only a one-and-a-half tone distance between its root and 3rd (D to F). This distance is called a *Minor* third and has a completely different emotional feel from the Major 3rd in C Major. Put simply, Minor 3rds feel sad and are the opposite of Major 3rds.

When we play the notes C D E F G A B C over a C Major chord, we subconsciously organise the scale from the root of the C chord and hear every interval in the scale in relation to the root C.

When we play the notes C D E F G A B C over a D Minor chord, we subconsciously organise the scale from the root of the D Minor chord and hear every interval in the scale in relation to the root D.

Because there is a different pattern of intervals in notes between C to C and D to D, the same notes create a very different feel.

The Major 3rd in Major and the Minor 3rd in Dorian are not the only differences in these two scales and in fact, every scale contains a different set of intervals.

To highlight and define the differences in scales, musicians compare the structure (step pattern) of a scale to the structure of the Major scale. The Major scale is the main building block of most music so it is considered a good 'base' that we can use as a reference.

The distance from one note to the next defines a scale's structure, for example, C to D, D to E, E to F, etc. The distance from C to D is a tone (two frets on the guitar), but the distance from E to F is only a semitone (one fret on the guitar). In any Major scale this pattern is *always*:

Tone, Tone, Semitone, Tone, Tone, Tone, Semitone.

This pattern is the 'DNA' of the scale. If this pattern changes, then it is no longer playing a Major scale.

As I mentioned, the Major scale is the building block of all music so its pattern is given the simple formula

1 2 3 4 5 6 7.

We now have a 'standard' that we can use to help us compare the characteristics of different scales.

The D Dorian mode begins on the second note of the C Major scale. The distance from D to E is a tone, but the distance from E to F is a *semitone*. We have already deviated from the Major scale pattern which begins with '*Tone Tone*'.

In fact, the Dorian mode has two notes that are different from the Major scale. Its formula is

1 2 b3 4 5 6 b7.

The Phrygian mode has four note that are different from the Major scale. Its formula is

1 b2 b3 4 5 b6 b7.

These different formulas, caused by the different patterns of tones and semitones are why modes all have different musical characters.

The best way to see these differences is to show the notes of the mode when they're played with the same root note.

Scale	Formula	Notes
C Major	1 2 3 4 5 6 7	C D E F G A B
C Dorian	1 2 b3 4 5 6 b7	C D Eb F G A Bb C
C Phrygian	1 b2 b3 4 5 b6 b7	C Db Eb F G Ab Bb

Due to the b3 in Dorian and Phrygian, these are considered 'Minor' modes, in that they produce a somewhat sad feeling when they're played in context. The Major scale has a natural or 'Major' 3rd producing its characteristic happy and triumphant feeling.

Each mode contains different variations to the Major scale formula and these variations create a unique musical feeling. One thing to take away from all this is that music is *very* manipulative. Watching a movie or TV show with different music playing in a particular scene can completely change the meaning of the action. Disney and Hollywood movies often 'tell' you how to feel or how to perceive a character on the screen by their music. Try muting your TV and playing a silly piece of music while watching an action movie. You'll be affected in a completely different way.

Manipulating an audience's perception in a movie is one thing, however, a worrying phenomenon to notice is how 'serious' news channels manipulate the audience's perception of events by using subtle music to reinforce their agenda and to 'tell' us how an event should make us feel.

Chapter Fourteen: All Scales and Modes

The following pages contain the most important scales and modes you should know as a modern guitarist. They are all given in five shapes and are shown with the correct anchor chords in the key of C. Your job is to learn to play all five shapes in the key centres of A, C, D, F and G in all five positions on the guitar.

This is a time-consuming process, so I strongly suggest that you take only one scale at a time and try to master it in all five keys in all five positions over the period of a week. Begin by learning the scale shapes around the chord anchors all over the neck in the key of C using the exercises in Chapter Ten and Eleven. Use the recommended backing tracks in each chapter to help you *hear* how each mode sounds and feels.

As you become confident playing these shapes in the key of C, move on to the ACDFG exercises taught in Chapters Eleven and Twelve. Work in one position each day and begin each day with a new position before recapping the previous day's practice. Remember, the sequence of practice steps is:

In the order of keys A, C, D, F and then G,

- Play the chord, ascend and descend the scale, play the chord. Say the chord names out loud

- Play the chord, descend then ascend the scale, play the chord. Say the chord names out loud

- *Visualise* the chord, ascend and descend each scale

- *Visualise* the chord, descend then ascend each scale

- Ascend one shape then descend the next

- Descend one shape then ascend the next

Work with a metronome to ensure your rhythm is consistent (especially when changing chord) before gradually increasing your speed.

The most common issue to slow students down is not knowing where the root notes are in each position. Make sure you have the root notes memorised on the neck before launching into the exercises.

These exercises are a big undertaking, but you will be a much better musician for having practiced them. Remember, while memorisation is the goal, there is only a certain amount of information that can be kept in our head at one time.

Above all, the end goal is to make music. When you're comfortable with playing the ACDFG scales in one position, try using each scale to play a melody on each chord instead of playing the scale. Using the 'two bars per key' backing track in each chapter, play a short musical line in the right key every time the key changes. This is quite a tough exercise because you should start your melodies in the *middle* of the scale, rather than at the top or bottom.

To learn to begin at any point in the scale, write short licks that begin on different notes of the anchor chord. When the key changes, quickly play the anchor chord and begin your lick from one of the notes in the chord and then gradually phase out the anchor chords.

There is no hurry to master the following material, but after working through this section over a period of weeks or months you will know your guitar neck inside out.

To help you organise your time, the scales that you should prioritise are marked with an *.

The Phrygian Mode

Formula 1 b2 b3 4 5 b6 b7

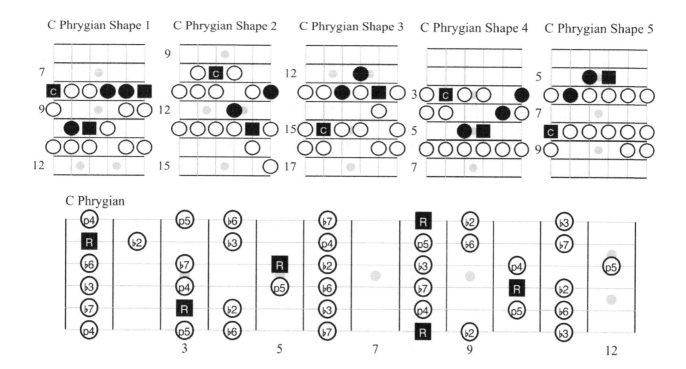

The Phrygian mode is a dark-sounding, Spanish flavoured mode that is popular with players such as Chick Corea and Al Di Meola. It is often used in heavier rock music and can be heard in many tunes by Metallica.

The Phrygian mode is identical to the Aeolian mode except that Phrygian contains a b2 scale degree. This b2 degree is responsible for the heavy Spanish flavour.

The ACDFG exercise can be practiced with the following backing tracks:

Backing track ten: Four bars per chord (Play the chord, ascend and descend each scale, play the chord).

Backing track eleven: Two bars per chord (Ascend and descend each scale).

Backing track twelve: One bar per chord (Ascend one scale, descend the next).

The Lydian Mode*

Formula 1 2 3 #4 5 6 7

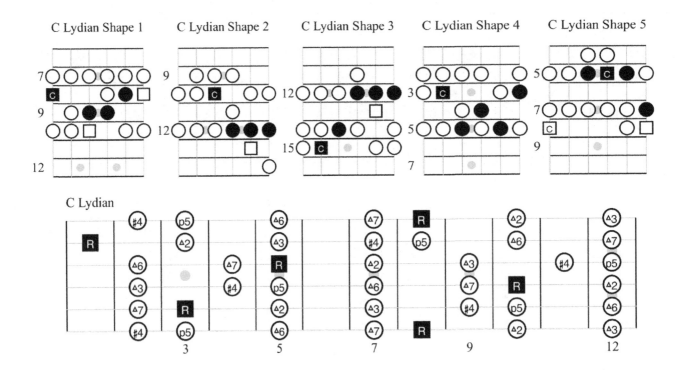

The Lydian mode is a Major sounding mode with one main difference from the traditional Major scale: the 4th degree of the scale is raised by a semitone. This seemingly tiny alteration to the Major scale creates an 'other-worldly' feeling and has been used with great results by musicians as diverse as Frank Zappa and Danny Elfman.

The ACDFG exercise can be practiced with the following backing tracks:

Backing track seven: Four bars per chord (Play the chord, ascend and descend each scale, play the chord).

Backing track eight: Two bars per chord (Ascend and descend each scale).

Backing track nine: One bar per chord (Ascend one scale, descend the next).

The Mixolydian Mode*

Formula 1 2 3 4 5 6 b7

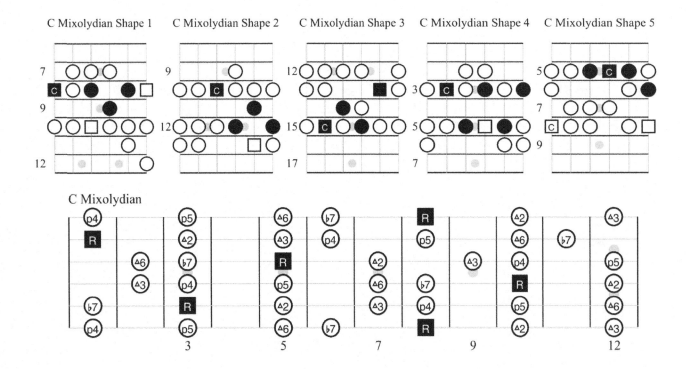

The Mixolydian mode is commonly combined with both Major and Minor Pentatonic scales. It is frequently heard in blues, rock and country guitar solos and very often heard in the playing of Derek Trucks, the Allman Brothers and Stevie Ray Vaughan. If you're listening to a 12 bar blues and the mood lifts from a Minor to a Major sound, this is often created by either using the Major Pentatonic scale or the Mixolydian mode.

The Mixolydian mode is identical to the Major scale, however Mixolydian contains a b7 interval, which takes some of the bright shine off the pure Major scale. By 'dulling down' the Major scale's brightness, Mixolydian becomes more suitable for upbeat rock and blues.

The ACDFG exercise can be practiced with the following backing tracks:

Backing track thirteen: Four bars per chord.

Backing track fourteen: Two bars per chord.

Backing track fifteen: One bar per chord.

The Aeolian / Natural Minor Mode*

Formula 1 2 b3 4 5 b6 b7

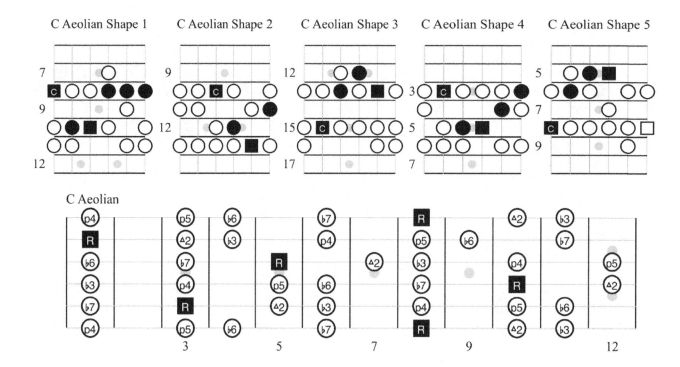

Aeolian is probably the most commonly used mode in heavy rock and metal. It is by nature a Minor mode as it contains a b3, however, the addition of the b6 creates a darker, heavier sound than the Dorian mode.

The Aeolian mode is also often used on Minor jazz-blues tunes.

Modern rock tunes often use the Aeolian mode, a classic example being Empty Rooms by Gary Moore.

The ACDFG exercise can be practiced with the following backing tracks:

Backing track ten: Four bars per chord (Play the chord, ascend and descend each scale, play the chord).

Backing track eleven: Two bars per chord (Ascend and descend each scale).

Backing track twelve: One bar per chord (Ascend one scale, descend the next).

The Locrian Mode

Formula 1 b2 b3 4 b5 b6 b7

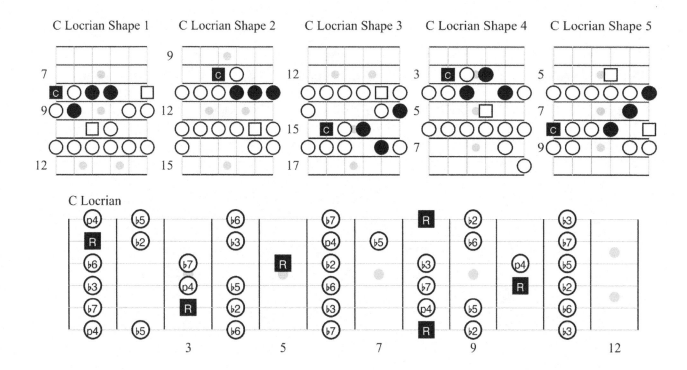

The Locrian mode is rarely used in popular music but crops up fairly often in death metal and heavier solos. Unexpectedly it is one of the most commonly used modes in jazz, and often occurs whenever you see a m7b5 chord.

Every note in the Locrian scale apart from the 4th is flattened so it almost is as far away from the Major scale as you can get. However, because our ears are used to hearing Major melodies and harmony, we are often tricked into subconsciously reorganising chord progressions so that we hear them as Major scale progressions.

In heavy metal, the Locrian mode is often played over power chords with a b5 to keep the harmony simple and let the melody of the scale define the tonal centre.

The ACDFG exercise can be practiced with the following backing tracks:

Backing track sixteen: Four bars per chord.

Backing track seventeen. Two bars per chord.

Backing track eighteen: One bar per chord.

The Minor Pentatonic Scale*

Formula 1 b3 4 5 b7

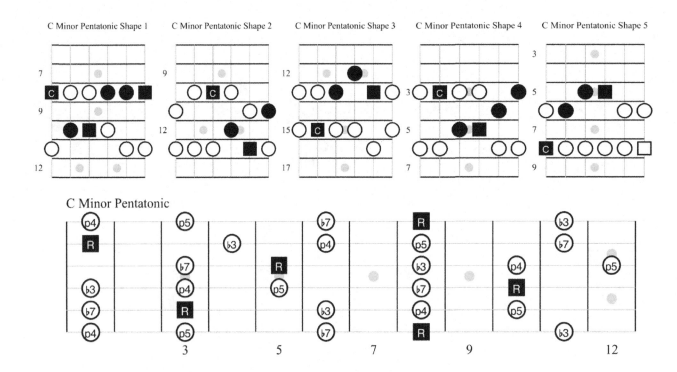

The Minor Pentatonic (blues) scale is the most ubiquitous scale in modern electric guitar music. I would estimate that over 80% of the classic rock solos are based around this important sound.

The Minor Pentatonic scale is normally the first scale that beginner guitarists learn, and quite rightly so. It is instantly accessible, easy to play and immediately lends itself to some of the most classic guitar licks ever recorded.

Essentially, the Minor Pentatonic scale *is* the sound of blues and rock. It can be played over Major and Minor keys and is extremely versatile.

The blues scale is created by adding an extra b5 note to the standard pentatonic scale. The extra b5 or 'blues' note unsurprisingly adds a more sombre, bluesy air to the sound.

The Minor Pentatonic scale has been used by literally everyone at some stage so it is pointless to list its main protagonists. Lightnin´ Hopkins, Jimi Hendrix, Jimmy Page, Eric Johnson and Paul Gilbert are all excellent examples of players who have treated the Minor Pentatonic scale in different ways.

The ACDFG exercise can be practiced with the following backing tracks:

Backing track ten: Four bars per chord (Play the chord, ascend and descend each scale, play the chord).

Backing track eleven: Two bars per chord (Ascend and descend each scale).

Backing track twelve: One bar per chord (Ascend one scale, descend the next).

With pentatonic scales, alter the rhythm you play in these exercises and use triplets instead of 1/16th notes to play through each scale.

The Major Pentatonic Scale*

Formula 1 2 3 5 6

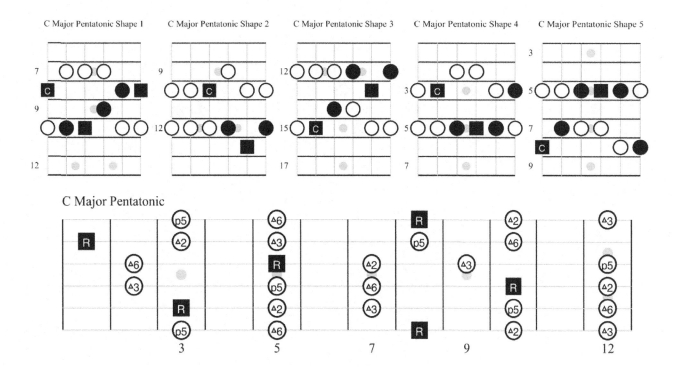

The Major Pentatonic scale is almost as widely used in modern music as its Minor cousin, however the brighter sound of the Major Pentatonic is less gritty and is often used in conjunction with the Minor Pentatonic scale to lift the music to more uplifting feelings.

The fingerings for the Major and Minor blues scales are identical, and the Major blues scale is often viewed as 'the same' as the Minor Pentatonic scale, but just starting three frets lower.

Stevie Ray Vaughan and Jimi Hendrix were masters of combining Major and Minor Pentatonic scales to create rich and complex emotions in their solos.

The ACDFG exercise can be practiced with the following backing tracks:

Backing track seven: Four bars per chord (Play the chord, ascend and descend each scale, play the chord).

Backing track eight: Two bars per chord (Ascend and descend each scale).

Backing track nine: One bar per chord (Ascend one scale, descend the next).

With pentatonic scales, alter the rhythm you play in these exercises and use triplets instead of 1/16th notes to play through each scale.

The Melodic Minor Scale*

Formula 1 2 b3 4 5 6 7

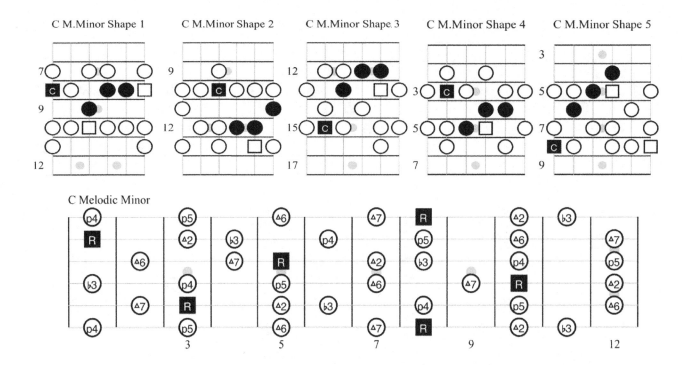

The Melodic Minor mode is one of the most commonly used Minor scales in both classical music and jazz. It has a rich, deep quality that transcends genres. The version of the Melodic Minor shown in this book would be more accurately described as the 'Jazz' Minor scale, or Ionian b3 scale because the true, traditional Melodic Minor scale from classical music is formed differently depending whether it is played ascending or descending.

The classical version of the Melodic Minor ascends as shown above, however it descends back to the root using the Aeolian mode. Most modern musicians do not distinguish between the ascending and descending versions of the Melodic Minor mode and will normally ascend and descend using the above pattern.

As mentioned, the Melodic Minor scale in this context can be better referred to as the Ionian b3 scale; it is identical to the Ionian (Major) scale apart from containing a b3 interval instead of a major 3rd.

The ACDFG exercise can be practiced with the following backing tracks:

Backing track ten: Four bars per chord (Play the chord, ascend and descend each scale, play the chord).

Backing track eleven: Two bars per chord (Ascend and descend each scale).

Backing track twelve: One bar per chord (Ascend one scale, descend the next).

The Lydian Dominant Mode

Formula 1 2 3 #4 5 6 b7

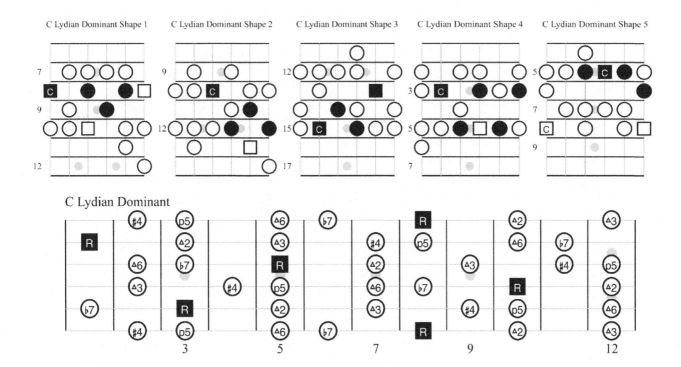

The Lydian Dominant mode is a common mode in jazz and fusion. It has a similar construction to the Mixolydian mode but has a raised 4th degree. It is normally used over dominant 7 chords, and most musicians tend to view the #4 degree as a b5, which is similar to the more common blues scale. For this reason, the Mixolydian, Blues and Lydian Dominant modes are often freely combined.

Lydian Dominant is often used on both static and functional (resolving) dominant 7 chords, and provides a great 'crossover' between traditional and jazzy blues.

The ACDFG exercise can be practiced with the following backing tracks:

Backing track thirteen: Four bars per chord.

Backing track fourteen: Two bars per chord.

Backing track fifteen: One bar per chord.

The Altered Scale

Formula:1 b2 #2 3 b5 #5 b7 (Normally seen as 1 b9 #9 3 b5 #5 b7)

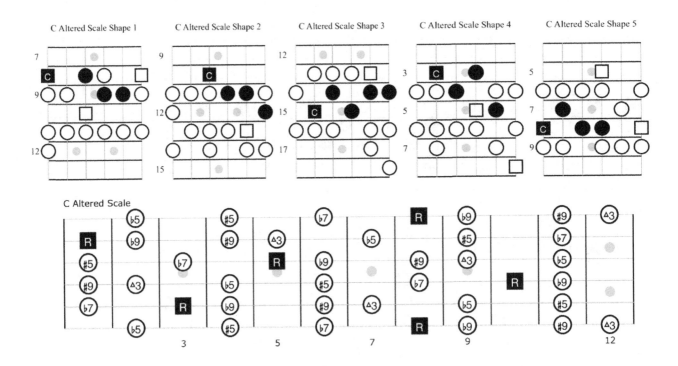

Definitely one for the real jazz players, the Altered or 'Super Locrian' mode comprises the root and guide tones of a dominant 7 chord (1, 3 and b7) plus *every* possible chromatic alteration to the dominant 7 chord (b9, #9, b5 and #5). It lends itself perfectly for use over an altered dominant chord that resolves to the tonic of the key, for example:

C7#5b9 - Fm7

Technically, theorists may say that it is more suited for use when the dominant chord resolves to a Minor tonic chord, but it is still commonly used when the dominant chord resolves to a Major chord.

It is important to note that the Altered scale does *not* contain a natural 5th degree, which gives it an extremely unsettled sound, but because it is normally used on functional dominant chords this characteristic can work beautifully.

This scale is often called the Super Locrian mode because it is identical to the Locrian mode, but contains a b4 (Major 3rd interval). For this reason, the Altered scale functions very differently and is considered a Major mode and is used over dominant-type chords.

The Altered scale can be used over a static altered dominant chord as shown in the following progressions, and while this is a very useful way to practice it to get to grips with its unique flavour, it is rare to see it used musically in this context.

The ACDFG exercise can be practiced with the following backing tracks:

Backing track nineteen: Four bars per chord.

Backing track twenty: Two bars per chord.

Backing track twenty-one: One bar per chord.

The Harmonic Minor Scale*

Formula 1 2 b3 4 5 b6 7

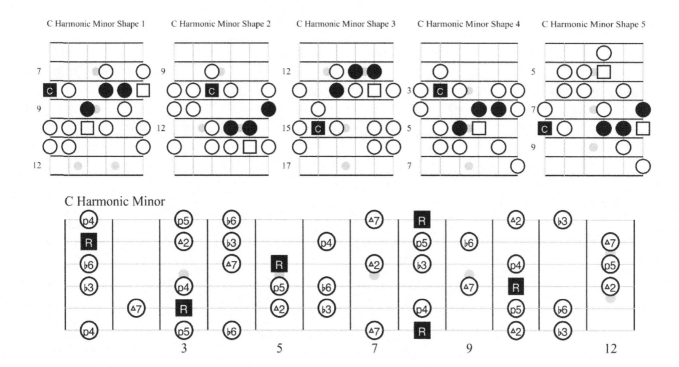

The Harmonic Minor scale can sound a bit old-fashioned these days, but if used sparingly, this unique flavour can add depth and intelligence to your solos.

The Harmonic Minor scale is characterised by the tone and a half jump between the b6 and the natural 7th degree, and instantly conjures up an Arabian/Middle Eastern ambiance. This is caused by the tone-and-a-half jump between the b6 and the natural 7th degree (Ab to B in the key of C).

Traditionally, the Harmonic Minor scale (true to its name) has been the source of Minor harmony and chord structure in classical music. Whereas pieces of music written in Major keys generally take their chords from the harmonised Major scale, pieces of music in Minor keys normally derive their chords from the harmonised Harmonic Minor scale.

The ACDFG exercise can be practiced with the following backing tracks:

Backing track ten: Four bars per chord (Play the chord, ascend and descend each scale, play the chord).

Backing track eleven: Two bars per chord (Ascend and descend each scale).

Backing track twelve: One bar per chord (Ascend one scale, descend the next).

The Phrygian Dominant Mode

Formula 1 b2 3 4 5 b6 b7

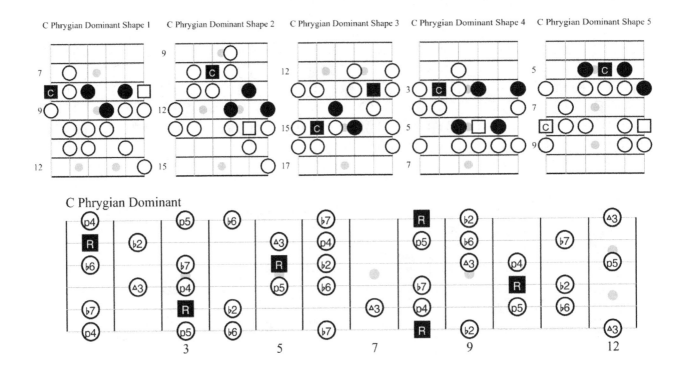

The Phrygian Dominant scale is extremely popular in both jazz and rock. It has a very Spanish, Gypsy quality to it, which makes it instantly recognisable.

Many people would consider that the Phrygian Dominant mode is the primary scale of most flamenco music.

In rock, it has commonly been used by Rush and Metallica, and used on the famous 'pick tapping' section of Joe Satriani's *Surfing with the Alien* (1:09).

The Phrygian Dominant mode is a favourite of neoclassical rock players such as Yngwie Malmsteen, as the tone-and-a-half step between the b2 and the Major 3rd instantly creates a bold classical feeling.

In jazz, the Phrygian Dominant mode is often used on a Minor ii v i. When played over a functional (resolving) dominant chord, Phrygian Dominant melodies strongly imply a resolution to the Minor tonic because the b6 degree of the Phrygian Dominant mode becomes the Minor 3rd of the tonic chord.

The ACDFG exercise can be practiced with the following backing tracks:

Backing track nineteen: Four bars per chord.

Backing track twenty: Two bars per chord.

Backing track twenty-one: One bar per chord.

The Half Whole (Diminished) Scale

Formula 1 b2 #2 3 #4 5 6 b7 (Normally seen as 1 b9 #9 3 b5 5 b7)

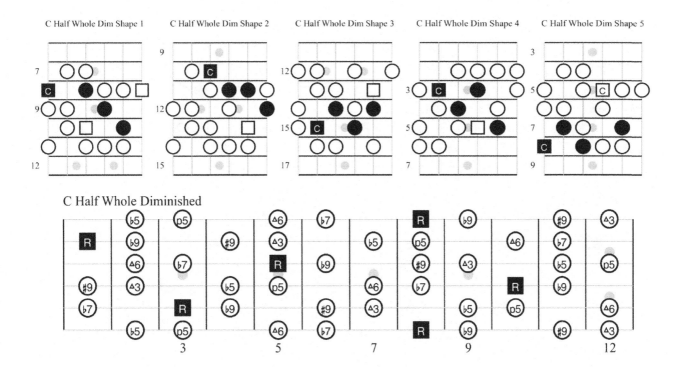

Synthetic scales are ones that do not occur 'naturally' in a modal system; they are created by using a particular repeating (synthetic) pattern of tones and semitones in their construction.

For example, the Half Whole Diminished scale is formed by following the pattern *half step, whole step, half step, whole step, etc.* Following this pattern generates an eight-note scale that lends itself heavily to playing melodic, 'geometric' patterns in solos. It is unusual to derive chords and harmony from synthetic scales, but it does sometimes happen in modern jazz and fusion.

The ACDFG exercise can be practiced with the following backing tracks:

Backing track nineteen: Four bars per chord.

Backing track twenty: Two bars per chord.

Backing track twenty-one: One bar per chord.

The Whole Tone (Augmented) Scale

Formula 1 2 3 #4 #5 b7

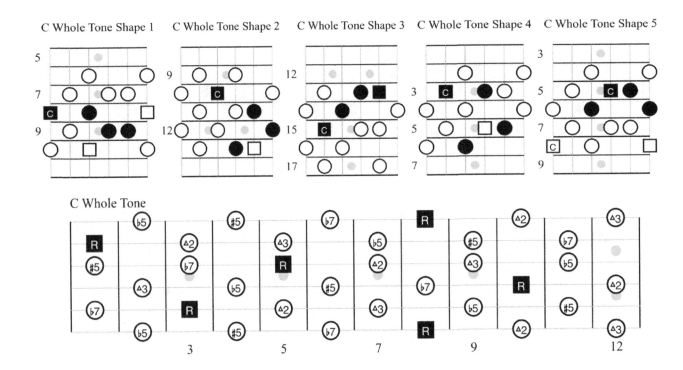

The Whole Tone scale is another synthetic scale. It is created by keeping a distance of one tone between *each* scale degree. The Whole Tone scale contains only six individual pitches, and due to its construction, there are only two transpositions of the scale.

The notes in C Whole Tone and in D Whole Tone are identical (this is easy to see on the full neck diagram above), so therefore just two transpositions cover every transposition the scale can be played in: C and C#. This is not to say that the Whole Tone scale can only be played in one key, it means that the notes in C, D, E, F#, G#, and A# Whole Tone are identical.

As a symmetrical scale, the Whole Tone scale, like the Half Whole Diminished scale, lends itself to 'geometric' musical lines and it is common to hear many sequences and patterns created from its structure.

The ACDFG exercise can be practiced with the following backing tracks:

Backing track twenty-two Four bars per chord.

Backing track twenty-three: Two bars per chord.

Backing track twenty-four: One bar per chord.

Conclusions and Practice Tips

This book contains a great deal of information that will probably take you many months or even years to work through, so my biggest piece of advice it to prioritise your practice goals. The exercises and scales in this book that you should prioritise are asterisked (*) so make sure that these are your priority each time you pick up your guitar.

I highly recommend focusing on only one scale, and only one of Chapters One to Four at a time, combining their practice heavily with a song or style of music that you are working on.

For example, if you were learning to play a heavy rock song, you may wish to focus on learning the Aeolian mode in all five positions and work through the most important sequences in Chapter One before moving on to the intervals in Chapter Two.

Another approach to practising the scales section of this book is to take one mode per week or per month and master the CAGED system positions before working through the melodic ideas in the earlier chapters with that mode.

However you choose to divide up the material here, remember that the end goal is not simply to run patterns at a fast tempo, it is to use these ideas to form new, creative melodies in your own improvisations.

Speed can be a useful goal to measure progress, but by the exclusive pursuit of speed on difficult sequences, it is easy to train your fingers to just run patterns when it is time to solo. The important factor when going from patterns to melodies is simply to break up the patterns and to leave space.

Combine the patterns you are working on with licks that you already know. Force yourself to play something different. It will sound obvious and forced when you start out, but gradually they will become a more natural part of your playing and blend in with the music that you are already making.

If I was to emphasise just one thing for you to take away from this book, it is that *everything* in here is about *ear training*. Practicing sequences, intervals, triads, arpeggios and scales opens up your mind by allowing you to hear new creative possibilities. You are literally being forced to play and internalise melodic ideas you wouldn't have played before.

These new ideas may not come out immediately in your playing, but as with any new vocabulary, they will be there, tucked away for when the creative part of you wants them to emerge.

Above all, make sure you spend time practicing any new melodic patterns in a creative and improvisational way.

Have fun!

Joseph

Appendix A: Three-notes-per-string Scale Shapes

Major Shapes:

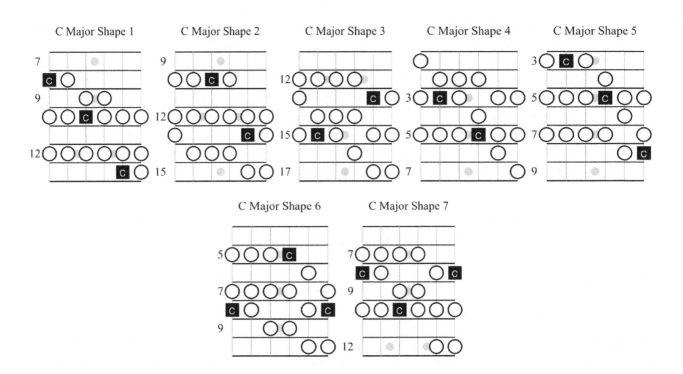

Melodic Minor Shapes:

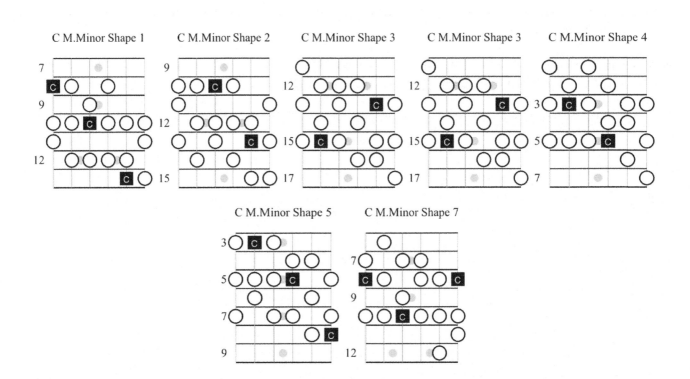

Harmonic Minor Shapes:

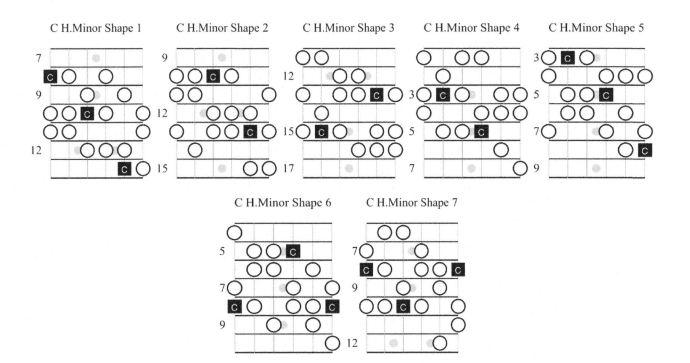

C H.Minor Shape 1 C H.Minor Shape 2 C H.Minor Shape 3 C H.Minor Shape 4 C H.Minor Shape 5

C H.Minor Shape 6 C H.Minor Shape 7

Made in the USA
Monee, IL
07 November 2020